KING REX AND THE COWBOY MAFIA

PHIL & SANDY HAMMAN
AND FRED BOFF

KING REX
AND THE
COWBOY
MAFIA

HISTRIA
PERSPECTIVES

Histria Perspectives

Las Vegas • Chicago • Palm Beach

Published in the United States of America by
Histria Books
7181 N. Hualapai Way, Ste. 130-86
Las Vegas, NV 89166 USA
HistriaBooks.com

Histria Perspectives is an imprint of Histria Books encompassing outstanding, innovative works meant to challenge and enlighten, as well as to inform and entertain, all while broadening the horizons of readers. Titles published under the imprints of Histria Books are distributed worldwide.

Library of Congress Control Number: 2024945347

ISBN 978-1-961689-74-9 (softbound)
ISBN 978-1-961689-73-2 (eBook)

DEDICATION

This book is dedicated to the memory of my wife, Ginger; our children, Suzie and Dave; their spouses Doug and Katie; and our grandsons, Tyler, Colby, Brady, and KJ. Without the support of my family, I could not have endured the life of a Special Agent. Beyond my family, I dedicate this book to the men and women who serve as Special Agents of the DEA, FBI, ATF, Secret Service, and dozens of other agencies whose members work tirelessly and risk their lives every day to keep America safe. Included among them was my friend and partner, Special Agent Everett Hatcher, who made the ultimate sacrifice for that very reason. They are the bravest of the brave and are the most loyal and committed Americans to walk among us. Without them, it is likely that the America we know and love would not exist.

Fred Boff

We dedicate this book to all past and current DEA Special Agents, especially those who have given their lives. It is also dedicated to the families who awaited the safe return of their loved ones at the end of each day.

Phil & Sandy Hamman

GINGER

Ginger and I began our incredible journey when we fell in love in college in the 1960s. For the next 47 years we were blessed by a truly remarkable marriage.

In 2012, our world changed dramatically when Ginger became seriously ill. The ensuing 4-year journey was something neither one of us expected, but life can be cruel, so you do whatever you can to continue the struggle. And Ginger certainly did whatever she could.

Our last 4 years were tough…but paled by comparison when measured against the first 43—decades filled with fun, hard work, lots of laughter, raising our family, and so many great times together. I once told Ginger that we won the war of the good years versus bad by an unfathomable margin.

When the journey ended on November 26th, 2016, I asked myself if we had been cheated because of Ginger's health problems and death? I answered with an emphatic No. Instead, I feel blessed—now and forever—for having shared a wonderful life, and for having obtained the love of an incredible woman.

Fred

NOTE TO THE READER

Much of *King Rex and the Cowboy Mafia* came from stories shared by retired DEA Special Agent Fred Boff, who was selected by DEA headquarters in Washington, DC, to be the Field Supervisor of what was a multi-state mobile task force. As such, he had control of all ordinary operational activities of the task force. Other information was obtained from investigative reports, court documents, evidence, and from recollections of people involved. The dialogue was created from evidence, those people involved, or how conversation would have been, based on written documents. *King Rex and the Cowboy Mafia* is a true story, and real names are used except in a few instances to protect the privacy or safety of certain individuals. The following are pseudonyms: Earl Simpson, Russell and Bonnie Moretti, Stevie Thomas, and Charlene Ray.

In the 1970s, marijuana and cocaine dominated the list of illegal drugs smuggled into the United States. In 1973, the Drug Enforcement Administration (DEA) was created to deal with America's growing drug problem. DEA Special Agents faced threats, death, and under-funded budgets, yet remained dedicated and driven to help America become a better place to live.

The line dividing good and evil cuts through the heart of every human being.
And who is willing to destroy a piece of his own heart?
—Aleksandr Solzhenitsyn

CHAPTER ONE

FLORIDA
January 23, 1977

HAROLD SIMS'S old pickup careened down a rutted lane through inky darkness, winding along back roads that skirted Florida's upper Gulf Coast and led to isolated fishing boat docks. Sims was familiar with the area, having been there to hunt and fish, and had brought good friend Douglas Hood and teen sisters Sheila and Sandy McAdams along. They had wine and beer and were scanning the area for one of the ample beach sites perfect for a secluded late-night party. Ahead, what appeared to be boat lights suddenly pierced the darkness. It was an odd time for a boat to be coming in unless something was wrong.

"Maybe those fishermen are broken down," Harold presumed. "Let's stop and see if they need some help."

At the end of the road, the shrimp boat *Gunsmoke* was just offshore. Unbeknownst to the four people in the pickup, smaller ferry boats scuttled sixty-pound bales of marijuana from the *Gunsmoke* to an empty beach along Sandy Creek. There were twenty tons of marijuana to unload—fresh from Colombia. Anticipating the possibility of rivals attempting to rob them of their drugs, one of the crew, Walter Steinhorst, was armed with a rifle and pistol. He was positioned down the road directly in front of two ten-wheel refrigerated trucks that would be used to transport the marijuana.

Anyone who knew Steinhorst would agree that he had a crazy temper and a reputation for unnecessary violence. He was a former member of the Outlaws motorcycle club and made others feel threatened even when he didn't intend to (though it usually was his plan to do so). Even friends considered his actions to be as vicious and calculating as a barracuda. The problem with crazy men, especially those in the smuggling business, is that they should never think. When they do, they often become paranoid, and paranoid people in the drug business get dangerous. Many years prior, the police had questioned him about a series of drug-related murders. Since they couldn't develop any hard evidence, they were forced to let him go. After that, Steinhorst joked about "getting away with murder." Likely, the comment was not made in jest.

Steinhorst was taking a break, huddled in a silver van to warm up from the drizzle and record-cold temperatures on this frigid night. He was built like a barroom bouncer. Stocky with a muscular five-foot-eight frame, he was not only overly confident but high strung and disturbingly paranoid. He poured a cup of steaming coffee from a thermos without taking his eyes off the road. When dim headlights broke through the steely gray blackness, Steinhorst swore, grabbed for his weapons, and threw the door open. Within moments, a pickup came into view and Steinhorst was already standing in the middle of the road waving his hands in the air and yelling, "Stop!"

Harold Sims, spotting the trucks and the shrimp boat, pulled past Steinhorst before easing over—with Steinhorst's pleas growing louder for Sims to stop. Harold rolled down his window, and Steinhorst appeared fuming, "Hey! This is a police operation. You can't be here tonight."

Douglas sat silently, staring straight ahead, but Harold surveyed the scene suspiciously. "We stopped to see if you were broken down and thought you might need a hand."

It was Steinhorst's job to protect the shipment of marijuana, and he was ready with an explanation. As a seasoned liar, he had no problem fabricating a story on the spot. "We're federal agents, undercover, and we made a big drug bust. We're unloading these bundles to be stored in an evidence locker. Turn around now and leave."

If Harold had accepted the explanation, an unnecessary chain of events would never have occurred. The four friends in the pickup would have left, partied the night away, and went on with their lives. But something about the hurriedness of the workers mixed with the scent of marijuana cutting through the cold wet wind and assaulting Harold's nostrils caused him to pause. A familiar face passed below the boat lights startling Harold, who instinctively yelled out, "Hey, I know you! I've seen you working at the Exxon on the beach. You aren't a federal agent."

It was true, one of the fifteen men unloading the drugs was very familiar to Harold, and he knew two other men there as well. This identification caused a noticeable shift in the demeanor of Steinhorst and the other men who paused nervously, sensing the situation was about to turn ugly. Steinhorst's eyes flashed anger. "Get out!" he shouted, brandishing a .38 in Harold's face.

By now, Steinhorst's accomplices, David Monroe Goodwin and Charles Hughes, had reached the pickup. Having come at a dead run from the beach, their rapid breaths in the chilled air billowed in white clouds under the glow of headlights.

Goodwin was panting heavily and came to an abrupt stop. "Who the hell are *they*?"

Rather than explaining, Steinhorst turned livid and started yelling threats, demanding that the men unloading drugs on the beach "get up here right now, damn it." Goodwin and Hughes tried calming him down, while Harold began squirming in his seat, then interrupted with a feeble explanation.

It was no use. Steinhorst had passed the point of logic and leveled his weapon straight at the passengers. Seconds later an echoing gunshot exploded, and Harold jerked then crumpled in his seat. Ronnie Ray, one of the men who had been unloading drugs, jumped when the loud shot went off. Harold twitched once then lay still, his eyes fixed and staring into the dark sky. Blood pooled around his body leaking slowly down the pickup seat.

Both girls screamed. Steinhorst turned momentarily away from the pickup, yelling to his men, some who ran off and some who were jogging toward the gunshot and commotion. Seizing the moment, Douglas threw open the passenger door and jumped out, running into the darkness with the two sisters right behind him. The three darted away from the pickup and into dense cover—deep rows of trees and bushes where they attempted to hide.

Following the gunshot, things along the beach went chaotic. There was shouting, the engine of the *Gunsmoke* revved up, and the disturbance caused one of the small ferry boats to slam into another. Goodwin ignored the mess going on around him and took matters into his own hands. He walked past Steinhorst who was continuing to bark orders, and strode to the edge of the tree line. Goodwin pulled his hood up. The icy air was becoming unbearable beneath a frigid black sky that soaked up any light that might have helped them find their way; the three escapees wouldn't get far.

"Come out! We're going to take your friend to the hospital, but we have to hurry."

The lie worked. Within a short time, Sandy, Sheila, and Douglas emerged, hopeful that they could get Harold to a hospital in time.

"Is he okay? Is he breathing?" one of the girls begged.

Steinhorst leveled the chrome-plated pistol toward Douglas who was the last to step from the trees and screamed at him and the two girls to, "sit your asses down and don't say another word."

Under the threat of the gun, the three did as they were told and crouched into a sitting position on the red clay road. Both girls looked to Douglas for reassurance.

Then Goodwin, his mouth dry from the stress of the situation, began yelling that he couldn't swallow. "Water!" he croaked, pointing to his throat and making gagging noises.

Ronnie Ray fumbled around in Goodwin's van and produced a thermos with unknown contents, which Goodwin gulped between what seemed to be dramatized gasps.

By now, more workers from one of the small ferry boats had come daringly close to the bloodied pickup to find out what was happening.

Steinhorst began verbally attacking them and yelling threats.

"Every damn person here is just as responsible as I am for this!" he said, pointing at the body in the pickup.

The two girls sat with their arms braided together, their sobs piercing the night. "What's going on? Are we going to be okay?" one of them pleaded to no avail.

No one dared to answer. Goodwin got a bundle of rope, and the captives' hands were bound tightly behind their backs while Steinhorst, still swearing, rummaged around in the van for bandanas or rags to use as gags. A nauseating panic rippled through Ronnie Ray. Though he could only see the man's eyes, he looked scared. The girls looked terrified, and their hysterical cries were only partially muffled by the gags. The three hostages were shoved into the van, and to their distress, Harold's lifeless body was thrown in next to them. When Steinhorst ordered all the men back to the beach, no one dared to argue with him. Douglas and the McAdams sisters sat in horrified silence for hours while bale after bale of the marijuana was loaded into the refrigerated trucks.

Hughes turned to Steinhorst and kept his voice low while pointing to the van. "We've got to do something about those witnesses."

Steinhorst just gave a nod of agreement. Ronnie Ray, who was still nearby, stood frozen, not knowing what to do or say. He noticed the familiar paranoia settling into Steinhorst's eyes, and hoped his own calming presence might have a positive effect. Steinhorst was looking right through him with a disturbing and vacant look as though Ronnie Ray weren't even there, which caused his legs to feel weak.

"What the hell are you looking at?" Steinhorst hollered.

Wordlessly, a dozen of the men continued unloading the bales as though nothing had happened. They worked through the night, some whispering with speculation about the future of the people restrained inside the van.

Adding to everyone's stress was the realization that when the crew on the *Gunsmoke* had heard the shot fired, they'd assumed something was terribly wrong and took off at full speed with 20,000 pounds of marijuana still below deck. Then one of the smugglers scuttled a ferry boat sending dozens of bales of weed bobbing around along the shore.

As the horizon began to lighten with the impending morning sun, the remaining men sent the refrigerated trucks off to the warehouse with whatever they'd been able to load into them. Adding to the mess of the operation, one refrigerated truck got stuck in mud despite the almost freezing temperatures. More backbreaking work was needed to free it. The crew of the *Gunsmoke* took the shrimper out to sea and (three days later) intentionally sank it with its hull still brimming with the marijuana they didn't have time to unload.

The van holding four unintentional intruders sat silent with only a dim grayness of early morning surrounding them. The lights of Panama City were miles away. The nightmare ahead was only beginning. Ronnie Ray inhaled a cold lungful of air. He could sense this was only going to get worse.

CHAPTER TWO

FLORIDA
1970s

PANAMA CITY SITS on the Gulf of Mexico in the Florida panhandle where the turquoise blue waters of the Atlantic meet the white sand beaches that stretch as far as the eye can see. By the 1800s, healthful sea baths and warm sunshine brought those seeking to improve various ailments such as arthritis. Eventually, as the community grew, the leaders christened it *Panama City*. The exotic-sounding name was chosen in hopes that it would spur real estate development and international trade due to its proximity to the Panama Canal. It became known as a center for fishing and boat building, and actively tempted tourists with promises of some of the world's most beautiful beaches. Scuba divers found adventure exploring the many shipwrecks in the clear ocean waters. In the 1970s, prominent businessmen and politicians came to conduct important meetings or hold conventions tantalizingly close to stunning beaches and clear waters. The popularity of Panama City brought in many new jobs, but the desolate miles of secluded beach line also paved the way for illicit drug smuggling.

It was along these coastal beaches that Carlos Gerdes and Jamie Holland thrived on the Florida nightlife. Gerdes was handsome and so determined in whatever he did, especially if it was cutting edge. His love of organic gardening—it was reported he'd work tirelessly to grow just one cucumber—must have seemed a natural stepping stone into the world of marijuana. His energy was balanced by Holland who was the strong, silent type.

It was in the early 1970s that they noticed the scarcity of pot, and finding it was a struggle when the supply would dry up, which it often did. One day while lounging restlessly on their twenty-eight-foot sailboat, they bemoaned the lack of available marijuana. The wind propelled them across peaceful waters beneath a glorious sky; the sound of water rushed past the boat creating a rhythmic lull. In spite of this, they yearned for a blissful joint to help them while away the hours.

They couldn't remember who first mentioned their proximity to Jamaica. From this seed sprouted the idea that they could easily sail to one of the small ports in the Caribbean, where marijuana was plentiful, and bring it back to Florida. Likely for a tidy profit. The long, lonely beaches, virtually uninhabited every night of the week, would make it safe for unloading. Soon the two men were rolling in cash as they pulled in drug load after drug load.

Then suddenly in mid-1975, the Jamaican marijuana supply dried up. The American government played a heavy hand in destroying this market. It didn't take long for the drug smugglers to sniff out the Colombian market though. But there was a caveat. The state of Florida had passed strict drug laws, which led Gerdes to look for a new home base. Gerdes had a lot to lose and wanted to protect the lifestyle he'd acquired and the image he'd built up as a suave business mogul who travelled in limousines and Lear jets. He gradually wanted to decrease the number of marijuana shipments unloading on Florida beaches. While in search of new locations, Gerdes happened to rub shoulders with a Tennessee millionaire by the name of John Ruppel, and a skinny Texan he at first only knew by the name "Muscles." Muscles reportedly worked for a wealthy Texas rancher with connections to politicians and bankers.

And after moving their enterprise to Texas, for a few precious years, Gerdes and Holland's operation would remain hidden.

CHAPTER
THREE

FLORIDA
1960s

RONNIE RAY HAD BEEN BORN in the mid-1940s to an unwed teenage mother whose family did not approve of this baby. Without support from her family, the young mother found herself on the streets, where she eked out a living for two years by sheltering in alleys and train stations. On cold nights, the two would huddle beneath a stinking blanket with Ronnie Ray clutched to her chest while she slept fitfully, worrying about being sexually assaulted or robbed of their meager possessions. The ugliness of the streets attached itself to Ronnie Ray like an invisible parasite. Neither future incarcerations nor self-loathing proved to remedy this lifelong affliction.

As much as his mother hoped that school would be his salvation for a better life, it was not to be. From the start, Ronnie Ray struggled with learning skills that seemed to come easily for the other students. He made efforts; he didn't want to disappoint the one person in his life who had always been there for him, his mother. But the academic road was not for him. The shame of hearing the snickering behind his back when he struggled to read words out loud, the daily mental exhaustion that nonetheless led to endless academic failures, the defeat of being handed another paper stamped with the familiar *F*. It would have been understandable if the humiliation he suffered had turned his heart to stone, but instead it had the opposite effect. Ronnie Ray refused to become hateful, and discovered that performing small kindnesses for others helped negate the bitter past. He tried and tried to succeed in school, but eventually the taunts and humiliation became too much. He dropped out in the eighth grade.

He was willing to work hard, and he tried this and that over several years. He discovered that in the adult working world, the compassion and integrity he'd developed during his torturous years as a student had blossomed into a strength. For the first time in his life, he felt not only accepted but well liked. People at work sought him out, invited him to join them for drinks after work, and regularly confided in him. Somewhere along the line it became customary for people to address him by his full name, Ronnie Ray, rather than just Ronnie. "It sounds like a down-home name," someone told him. "Like Bobby Joe or Billy Bob." It was a welcome change. Still, he could never quite obtain just the right job that earned him the pay or status he yearned for. In fact, he could never get life quite right, and as a young man dabbled in petty crimes.

He hit gold when he found Charlene. She was loving and down-to-earth and demanded a level of accountability from Ronnie Ray that he found comforting. She was confident without being uppity, and didn't believe in drinking or meanness. The latter wasn't a problem for him, but the drinking…

Charlene craved the good life, which by her measuring stick meant a solid trailer house, the absence of letters in the mailbox threating to turn off the water or electricity due to unpaid bills, and some weekend nights out with friends.

"I know you spent that money at the bar, Ronnie Ray," she accused him when they came up short on the rent.

"I joined the guys for one drink, Charlene. Damn. A man can't have a life and be married to you?"

"You sound just like my dad. You figure out where that money went and fast." She pointed to their son watching television in the other room and whispered, "I will not move him from school to school because his dad drank the rent away."

Ronnie Ray's blood went cold. That was how he'd been raised, and had vowed not to let the same happen to his beloved son. And snowballing out of control, one night of pilfering car parts turned into a weekend of fencing some stolen goods, which led him to some thugs who needed a mule to run drugs for them. He justified each illegal deed by reasoning that it put food on the table for his wife and young son. With a day job in a local Panama City factory, the petty crimes on the side helped financially.

One chance evening in a local rundown bar, one of the few places he felt welcome, Ronnie Ray unexpectedly started down a much wider criminal path—one with too many twists and turns for him to see what was actually waiting down the road. He sat in his dirty work clothes, ragged jeans, and a worn t-shirt, downing the cold beer he felt he'd rightfully earned after a physically exhausting week of hard labor. At six-foot-two and 190 pounds, most of his friends thought he looked more like an aging California surfer than a mill worker. This morning, Charlene had rather forcefully reminded him about two overdue bills, and that their twelve-year-old son needed new shoes. He loved the boy more than anything and strived to raise and protect him with the same care and concern his mother had for him years ago. Guilt settled like a rock in his stomach. The family's one car made a horrible grinding sound whenever he put on the brakes, so he tried gauging his speed to avoid having to slow down or make stops. Perhaps he should have gone home straight from work, but the daily demands of life were weighing him down, and sometimes a man just needed a night without worries. As if on autopilot, he found himself at this favorite hangout.

Ronnie Ray's buddy tapped his arm excitedly. "Hey, I've got something goin' on that I can let you in on if you're game for some quick cash. No lie man," the friend added in a hushed whisper. He pulled a roll of bills out of his pocket and quickly waved it with a flourish in front of Ronnie Ray's face. Ben Franklin's somber image was clearly visible on the wad of cash even under the dim lighting of the bar. Ronnie Ray perked up and took a deep breath, sucking in a lungful of the familiar air soaked with stale cigarette smoke. Eager to hear more, he leaned forward to hear better over the sound of Johnny Cash's voice pounding out "Ring of Fire" from the nearby jukebox.

"Ronnie," the friend said in a cautious way that indicated he could only share this with a trusted comrade, "for basically no effort and a few hours of your time, you can pick up an easy *five grand*." He paused to take in Ronnie Ray's initial reaction, which, based on the widening of eager eyes seemed to be a positive one. So he quickly added, "There's a little risk, but it's a good business opportunity if you're smart about it." He knew the hook was firmly in Ronnie Ray's mouth, and all he needed to do was give it a little tug.

"Tell me more," Ronnie Ray said, trying not to sound too eager.

"I've done this before. All I do is help load a van with pot and drive her up to the New York area or some other places. When I get back, there's five grand tax-free cash waiting for me. We need more manpower though. It has to be loaded and delivered fast."

Ronnie Ray took another swig of beer while he processed the idea in mind. *Five thousand for a drive up the coast.* Hell, he had to work months busting his ass at the thankless paper mill to make that much. *This could help my son. My family.* Besides, Ronnie Ray didn't have a terrible record, so if he got pinched, the judge might be lenient, he convinced himself. The hook was set. With vibrations pulsing from the jukebox, Ronnie Ray soaked up this rare moment of hopefulness and dared to imagine a better future. He'd help out just this one time, and that would be it.

Charlene had dissolved into tears when a policeman had shown up at their house with a warrant to search Ronnie Ray's car. Nothing came of it, but she knew he wasn't just "out with the guys" like he claimed when he was actually delivering a few dozen pounds of pot around the area.

"Do you even think about our son?" she'd accused him. "Do you want kids at school to make fun of him because his dad's in jail? Or worse!"

He argued with her at first, but she was adamant.

"Get a second job, work overtime, whatever! Hell, I'll get a second job." If we need more money, there's a better way, Ronnie Ray. If you go to jail again, I *will* divorce you, so make your decisions wisely!"

"I promise, Charlene. You gotta believe me. My family means everything to me." And after just one more quick job, he'd leave the criminal life behind for good.

CHAPTER FOUR

RONNIE RAY HAD HELPED UNLOAD many shipments of pot since his buddy first told him about this "business" opportunity over a year ago. But tonight, while working on this particular load from a shrimp boat named *Gunsmoke*, things had gone terribly wrong. Then, to Ronnie Ray's shock, Steinhorst ordered him of all people into the van loaded with three bound captives. Ronnie Ray's lips felt thick, and his legs resisted moving, but he managed to haul himself into the van. He turned and whispered to the girl closest to him who seemed to be the taller of the two, "Don't worry, you'll be fine. You'll be home soon." Both girls' sobs lessened noticeably. He hoped he was telling them the truth. If he could have done so without Steinhorst realizing, he would have bolted out and made his way back into town.

Steinhorst was a sociopath who wouldn't think twice about adding another dead body to the list. Ronnie Ray's mind twisted thinking of the exact wording that might encourage Walter Steinhorst to not make the situation worse, something he'd seen him do in the past. Steinhorst had warmed up to Ronnie Ray; there was something about the younger man's humbly honest personality that drew others into his circle, even a crazed killer like Steinhorst.

Finally Ronnie Ray mustered up the nerve to talk to this paranoid man who had been pacing around the van with the dead body in it, and glowering at anyone who came near. "Let's take them farther out and let them go. By the time anyone finds them, we'll be long gone. Besides, these three look too scared to say anything." There were muffled sounds of desperation from the three captives, and Ronnie Ray felt the nausea flood his stomach.

Steinhorst worked his jaw for a few seconds biting on the inside of his cheek, then responded with the unconvincing nod of someone who didn't really agree and climbed into the driver's seat with Hughes next to him.

Between the van rattling down the rutted road, and the sounds of heavy breathing from the three captives in the back, Ronnie Ray felt the nausea flood his stomach. *Where the hell is he dragging us?* The "if onlys" tapped at his brain: if only those kids hadn't stopped, if only he hadn't agreed to help unload the boat… This was supposed to be one of the last times he was ever going to help with a drug job. Tomorrow was his day to turn over a new leaf. To just get the hell out of this side job. Now the whole thing had taken a bad turn.

Without warning, Steinhorst swerved to the side of an empty building and made a lengthy call from a pay phone booth. There seemed to be more stops, more phone calls by Steinhorst, and more seemingly endless driving. The whole day had gone by. The day was agonizing hell for Ronnie Ray, and he could only imagine what the captives were going through.

Steinhorst and Hughes discussed where to take their "cargo." Hughes suggested that they give the witnesses money to keep their mouths shut. Steinhorst had other ideas. They debated various options. They argued. And then eventually picked a location. It was an area they were familiar with near Perry, 125 miles away. By the time they finalized what to do and had driven circuitous routes, the whole day had gone by. The sun was dropping in the west, and twilight was upon them.

After one last phone call, Steinhorst returned in a surprisingly carefree mood and turned to the captives. "We're taking you into the woods. Deep. When we let you out, you're going to sit there until sunrise, and then you can walk yourselves out." Whether this convinced the silhouetted figures tied and gagged was uncertain. It didn't completely convince Ronnie Ray. Although it had been his idea to turn them loose, he had a continued bad feeling. The captives had seen their friend get shot, could identify one of the workers, and now had seen the inside of Goodwin's meticulous custom van. Powerless to do anything against Steinhorst, Ronnie Ray sat motionless while the van rolled on to the next destination that only Steinhorst knew.

With the night now black, he turned down a lonely stretch of road that led to an old hunting lodge. A discussion exploded in the van between Steinhorst and Hughes, focusing on the fate of the three passengers. Steinhorst became uncontrollable—screaming, swearing, and swinging his rifle around recklessly. *"You'll all damn well be dead if you try to cross me!"* he raged every time Hughes tried to reason with him.

Finally, Steinhorst threw open the door of the van. *"Get out!"* he barked, grabbing the arm of the nearest girl and yanking her out as she stumbled to keep her balance. The other two followed hesitantly and all were marched through thick vegetation of sand pines, ferns, and scrub brush. The moon had broken through clouds casting just enough light to give Ronnie Ray the impression of watching a black-and-white horror movie.

After a quarter mile, they stopped near a large sinkhole, a small lake created when ground buckled. It was one of hundreds that dotted the Florida countryside. Steinhorst's agitation revealed itself in the way he snapped at Hughes. He was talking rapidly with disjointed speech—starting a thought and then jumping to some paranoid conclusion. "Let's get this over with. Get them over here," he ordered Ronnie Ray. Though why it was his job to be Steinhorst's pawn he didn't know or dare to ask. Ronnie Ray went pale, and Steinhorst's face started to contort. With Hughes's help, Ronnie Ray led the three living witnesses to the lake's edge then stood back.

With a shove to Douglas Hood's shoulder, Steinhorst smirked and ordered all three to kneel. Steinhorst's sadistic side had emerged, and he was enjoying his control over the captives. Both girls were sobbing hysterically from under their gags. Desperately, one of the girls glanced at Ronnie Ray and pleaded to him with her eyes. Desperate eyes. Her uncontrollable shaking left him with ice in his stomach. Ronnie Ray sickened thinking she thought he'd betrayed her. Steinhorst had promised to let them go, but Ronnie Ray knew that wasn't going to happen. He mustered up the nerve to say something. "Hey," he started with a slight croak to his voice, "let's pay 'em money to keep—"

An explosive *bang* split the night and echoed off the trees. At the same moment Ronnie Ray gasped, Douglas Hood slumped forward. A hole in the back of his head oozed a thick band of blood, and splatters hit Sandy's brown rabbit fur coat, staining it with crimson spots. Ronnie Ray's ears were ringing from the shot, and he could smell the gunpowder as it hung in the thick night air.

"What the hell?" Ronnie Ray took several nervous steps back while the two girls hopelessly scooted away from the lifeless body to avoid the flowing blood moving toward them.

Steinhorst didn't move, his pistol still leveled at Hood's bleeding head before swinging it toward the girls who cowered back. "You two are pretty hot," he said taking a step toward them. The girls cringed, and Steinhorst took another step forward. And so it continued, with Steinhorst clearly enjoying the fear he induced in the girls. "I could take you back to the lodge and have a little fun." He paused to gauge their reaction and smirked at the sound of their labored breathing as they hyperventilated beneath the gags. "I don't want anyone to say that Walter Steinhorst is unfair. So, I'll give you two minutes to think about what you would do so I let you live."

Tears rolled down the sisters' faces.

CHAPTER
FIVE

NEW YORK
Early 1970s

TWELVE HUNDRED MILES away from the swaying palm trees of sun-kissed Panama City, the cement jungle of New York City was just waking up to a chilled morning. Its towering skyscrapers stretched upward as if in competition to see which would be the first to touch the hazy sky. The looming buildings all but blocked any chance of the dim morning light reaching the sidewalks. The city is home to a diverse population of millions, and among the multitudes, Fred Boff, a twenty-nine-year-old drug enforcement Special Agent, was bogged down in traffic as he drove to work. Boff, six-foot-six and athletically built, with huge basketball player hands, was cocooned in his car as he was every morning while waiting to emerge a DEA agent—that was if he ever managed to make his way across Manhattan. He cracked two windows, encouraging a cross breeze to clear out a burst of diesel fumes clouding the car. The smell of greasy food frying mingled with vehicle tailpipe exhaust assaulted his nose. As the clogged traffic from New Jersey slowed once he entered the city, he used the idle time to run through the day's agenda. Blaring horns from the traffic jam did little to distract his focused concentration.

Work in drug enforcement was a career he prized, except for the violence, which he was never able to accept as just "part of the job," even though it went hand-in-hand with illegal drugs. He thrived on working with a partner or team of agents, even if it meant going undercover, something he was never entirely comfortable doing. The clean-cut Fred felt he was better suited as a poster boy on a recruitment ad for the feds. Teamwork, however, flowed naturally from his days as a standout basketball player in high school and college; it was deeply embedded in his character. He told people that he was "blessed with athletic talent and was fortunate enough to attend college on a basketball scholarship." He'd grown up on the Jersey shore, and although his dad was a dentist, he had five siblings, so the scholarship was a godsend.

He finished two years of college at two different institutions before deciding the academic life wasn't for him. He'd been loading freight cars for a dollar an hour back home when he got a call from the coach at a nearby college wondering if Fred wanted to enroll and play basketball.

"Nope. I'm done with college," Fred said adamantly.

The director was undeterred. "We are unique among other colleges in that we have eight female students for every male student on campus."

Fred rubbed a swollen bruise on his arm that he'd acquired at work and briefly mulled over the director's words before proclaiming, "I can be there this afternoon!"

Later that day, the director showed Fred around campus and asked what he wanted to major in.

Drinking? Jump shots? Fred pondered.

"We have an opening for a transfer student in math, science, or English."

Fred immediately eliminated math and science. "English it is! I'm practically fluent in that language."

That fall while in college, basketball hadn't been Fred's only interest. When a bubbly cheerleader named Ginger caught his eye, he focused on this new goal.

"Let's go out this Friday," he encouraged rather than asked, trying a new tactic, since she'd turned him down the last several times he'd attempted to get a date.

Ginger flipped her hair to the side and smiled with weary exasperation. "Why would I ever think about going out with you?"

Fred, who was quick with wit, responded in his typical upbeat manner, "Because I'm cute, adorable, and fun to be with!"

Ginger shook her head, turned, and walked away. But the determined basketball player still didn't give up. He bought a small stuffed dog, attached a note that read "I'm even cuter than him," and placed it on Ginger's car. Two days passed, and as Fred approached his own car he noticed the stuffed dog sitting on the hood. Curious, he picked it up and saw a different note attached that read, "You are definitely not cuter than him." But Fred's efforts did not go to waste. He and Ginger dated through college. In addition to his confident outgoing personality, she found herself charmed by his even temper and the fact that he never displayed anger around her. Fred reminded Ginger that this quality more than made up for his sarcastic wit (and even that he saved for those who truly deserved it). After college, they married.

As a drug enforcement Special Agent, Fred was frequently pulled away from home for days on end. He was already being fast-tracked for a career advancement, and this required him to have diverse experiences. Since Fred's supervisor had him targeted for a promotion, Fred couldn't turn down an undercover assignment he'd have rather passed up. The case involved a man who was considered highly dangerous, but Fred rarely felt nervous about approaching such people. Not anymore. As a young child he'd been considered timid. The word "wimpy" may have been used on occasion. As he'd grown into a preteen, he'd become tall, skinny, and self-conscious. He'd begun playing basketball at the YMCA; based on his height, people expected him to be a natural, but Fred discovered he was easily intimidated by others on the court.

"I don't want to take a shot. I'll miss," he finally admitted to his dad.

His dad, who was known for being ready with a helpful and philosophical answer replied tenderly, "If you're afraid of failure, you can never succeed. I know you will miss shots."

Fred stiffened, not expecting that answer.

His dad continued. "You have to face up to the fact that sometimes you'll fail in life. You have to remember, the greatest baseball players are only successful about every one out of three times at bat. They fail two out of three times."

Fred took the advice to heart and discovered he was a natural not only at confronting difficult situations, but at basketball, where he went on to score 1,000 points during college. He drew on his dad's advice as he prepped to face this next opponent. As with most investigations, it began with a tip from an informant, Ed "Skull" Murphy who was not only a career criminal but a onetime professional wrestler. Skull had connections to a man named Michael Umbers.

"Check out my story," Skull said, displaying both hands in the air as if he had nothing to hide. "Umbers distributes more LSD in this country than any one you'll find, and," Skull leaned in lowering his voice, "he's the biggest producer of gay porn."

"I know the name," Fred replied coolly. Umbers had connections to the Mob. "Can you introduce me to his associates?" As tempting as it was to move straight to the intended target, undercover work took more finesse and time. Fred had to infiltrate a criminal group in the same way any wannabe off the street would or he'd come across as too obvious in his intentions. He had to start at the bottom, gain trust from the lower-level people, and then go after "The Big One." This was the reality of undercover.

What Fred didn't tell Skull was that the DEA had been looking for an insider to help them link Umbers to the nearly fatal shooting of mob boss Joseph Colombo. They knew Umbers was connected to Jerome Johnson, the triggerman in the shooting, who was then himself shot to death immediately after the attempted assassination.

Umbers was drawn like a fly to the filth of New York's illegal underbelly. Besides being a likely assassin, he was suspected of being behind the Stonewall Riots, the first attempt by the city's gay community to rise up against police raids. Stonewall was a gay bar, and on a serendipitous night in 1969, the patrons battled police in a raid and unknowingly setting off the gay rights movement. However, only a few short years had passed since the remarkable night, and attitudes were slow to change. So Umbers was a wanted man for many reasons, but so far they hadn't been able to pin anything on him to make an arrest.

So it was due to this new operation that resulted in Ginger arriving home to find Fred surveying himself with uncertainty in front of a full-length mirror dressed in a pair of tiny tight pink shorts and a fishnet shirt.

She looked him up and down with tempered curiosity. "I sure hope you're going to a costume party," Ginger said, not even needing to ask the reason behind the outfit. She quickly added, "And if *any* of our friends see you like that, I'll divorce you."

"It's kind of a party!" Fred replied enthusiastically. "I'm going to the gay pride parade." He turned to reveal a rather amateurish job of having applied some of Ginger's light blue eye shadow. "Can I bring this with me?" He held up a tube of glossy pink lipstick. "It keeps coming off. Hey, I even have a flag to carry in the parade, but you know how the job is. I can't tell you anything else other than our target is part of the gay community, so I have to look the part."

"Sounds dangerous," she offered.

"I like a challenge." There were many unexpected dangers in the job that for obvious reasons he didn't reveal to Ginger. Every new case seemed to bring some new risk. New York had strict sodomy laws that wouldn't be repealed until the 1980s. The gay community regularly came under attack and people were often caught between wanting to report being victimized, which carried the risk of being arrested for being gay, or letting the incident go unreported. Because of all this, people got away with violent acts, and now Fred was going under-cover dressed in drag.

Fred and his partner, Ron, whom everyone would eventually refer to as "Felix," needed to fit in. This meant dressing in the same tight pants and revealing shirts that were customary in the Village. They made a believable couple based on the opposites-attract theory. Standing five-foot-ten, Ron was handsome with his long blond hair and fastidious appearance. He was single and spent his free time perfecting various soup recipes that he brought to work to share with the other Special Agents. And his desk was spotless. Once while he,

Fred, and some other agents were executing a search and arrest warrant for cocaine on the lower east side, they found themselves in a filthy apartment. The suspects sat handcuffed on a grimy couch while agents searched the rooms.

"This place is a dump. I'm surprised Ron didn't put a chemical suit on for protection," one of the agents joked.

"Where the hell is Ron anyway?" Fred asked. The others shrugged and Fred went in search of his partner whom he found in the kitchen. "Hey, you gotta see this!" he called to the other agents who came scurrying to see what evidence might have been found. Instead they scrambled into the kitchen to find Ron wearing an apron and scrubbing the counter.

"What the hell are you doing?" Fred asked mystified.

"This place is a pigsty. I'm cleaning it up," Ron replied matter-of-factly. His compulsive need to clean could have been a problem had he scrubbed away evidence. Fortunately, he scoured a section of the kitchen that had no evidence related to the case.

And it was from this incident that Ron earned his nickname Felix, from the popular television sitcom *The Odd Couple*. One of the characters, Felix, was a neurotic neat freak who fancied cooking.

So, Fred and Felix posed undercover as lovers and repeatedly went out at night for nearly a year (often having quite a good time!) to fit in with the crowd, gain trust, and find out information. Fred was blessed with the ability to fit in easily. In school, his teachers had referred to him as "a talker," but it was this same verbal strength that led to his penchant for telling stories. People felt at ease with him; he told hilarious stories, which led the regulars in the Village to feel they knew and could trust him. He made friends with some of the kindest people he'd ever met, as well as his share of oddballs—a typical New York mixture. One of these was Big Tiny, who was considered to be one of Umbers's closest associates. Standing six-foot-three and weighing upwards of four hundred pounds, Big Tiny made no effort to hide the crush he had on Fred.

"If I was straight, I'd have it made," he bragged to Fred. "Every woman I meet in New York City practically begs me to sleep with her. It's tiring having to turn them away! They all want a big guy."

Michael "Dirty Mike" Umbers, forty-one years old, was the target of their investigation and another of the people who soon accepted the couple into his circle. Umbers reportedly owned a bar that offered prostitution on the side, and he also published a magazine that specialized in advertising to those looking to hook up with young boys. His associate Lance ("no last names, please") took a special liking to Fred. He bought Fred extra drinks, cozied up to him, and sought him out the minute he walked into the bar each night. This went on for many evenings until Felix finally came to Fred's rescue. "Lance, Lance, keep it in your pants! He's *my* guy," Felix gushed.

Fred and Felix were undercover as a couple, but Lance didn't play by the rules or respect boundaries. He continued hitting on Fred, but also was privy to details about Umbers. To call Umbers a shady character would be a grievous understatement. Umbers had been described by the New York police as a front man for the Carlo Gambino mafia family. It was in his capacity as the operator of an afterhours club frequented by the Gambino family that had originally linked him to the assassination attempt on the infamous Joseph Colombo. He wasn't someone to turn your back on.

And Umbers was brutal. Unstable. Umbers was gay, and he used Skull to set up rendezvous for him with rich doctors and businessmen who were desperate to keep their lifestyle shrouded in secrecy. Umbers's anonymous lover for that night would arrive at an out-of-the-way motel after dark, looking over his shoulder with paranoid vigilance. The stigma of a gay lifestyle would surely spell the end of any successful career. Often the evening went as expected, and both men left fully satisfied. But Umbers was conflicted. Sometimes for no apparent reason he'd brutally beat his paramour, who wouldn't dare report the crime for fear of being outed as gay.

Eventually though, the Special Agents made headway into understanding Umbers's LSD operation. Still lacking the hard evidence necessary for a bust, they continued unveiling names and gathering intel on the drug connections. Then they made a few small purchases of LSD to demonstrate their "trustworthiness."

"Come on, I have a treat to show you," Umbers said unexpectedly one night. They threaded their way through the crowd then Umbers escorted Fred out the door of the night club with Felix and Big Tiny following along. Fred expected to see an expensive car sitting along the street outside the bar or some such thing.

"Stay here," he stage-whispered and pressed one hand against Felix's chest to indicate he shouldn't go another step. "This is something for Fred's eyes only."

Umbers motioned for Fred to walk farther down the street. Big Tiny trailed behind, huffing and puffing loudly to keep up. Fred was rarely terrified, but the stories of Umbers beating men practically to death rolled through his head. There were other reasons, not the least of which was that Felix was the only one of them with a gun.

As they moved farther down the block and then to the next one, the noise from the crowded bars dampened, and the once bustling streets were empty, save for the broken bottles and assorted litter. Soon it was only the three of them. Fred wiped the sweat from his upper lip and side-eyed Umbers to gauge his expression. *It didn't feel right.* The sidewalks were void of people, and the buildings surrounding them were mostly empty warehouses.

"Where's the treat you're going to show me?" Fred asked calmly, hiding his anxiety and trying not to focus on the foreboding echo of their footsteps on the deserted sidewalk.

"Oh, just down here." Umbers pointed to a metal door looming a few dozen yards away, which didn't give Fred much reaction time. The building resembled an abandoned factory. There was no turning back now, and there wasn't really any choice but to be led inside. If he acted scared or refused to follow, it would arouse suspicion, and he couldn't risk damaging all the inroads that had been made through long hours of undercover work over an entire year. Fred's thoughts went to his gun, which was in the car due to being unable to conceal it anywhere in the skimpy clinging clothes he wore to fit in.

Fred steeled his nerves to stay sharp. Umbers took out a key, groped for the handle in semidarkness, and opened the rusty iron entrance door after which the trio stepped inside to a darkness that was all-consuming.

"Now the fun begins," Umbers murmured into the void.

Umbers switched on a light. They were in a stuffy tall-ceilinged hallway with dirty carpet sprinkled with cigarette butts. Umbers made small talk, and Fred followed him to an industrial elevator that lifted them up into the aged factory. If ever something felt "off," this was the time. The back of his neck prickled. He side-eyed Big Tiny to see if his face revealed any secrets, but Big Tiny merely responded with a straight face and a wink. It seemed as though Fred's heart was pounding so loudly that certainly Umbers and Big Tiny could hear each fear-laden thump. Fred tried to calm himself by playing through the possible outcomes in his head, deciding various options he would have, depending on what happened next.

Finally, the gears on the elevator ground to a screeching stop. The car jerked and then thudded to a stop. Fred remained alert to every detail and noticed faint sounds (curiously, it seemed like laughter) and the vibrations of a drum coming from the other side. The thick metal doors shuddered open and bright lights revealed a large brightly lit room of the brick-walled building. Laughter mixed with loud music billowed into the dim elevator. In the corner was a king-size bed surrounded by tungsten lights of various sizes and a massive video camera mounted on a sliding tripod. Atop the bed, two naked and well-oiled men wrestled about and were very obviously in a state of sexual arousal. A man with a microphone was standing next to the video camera. Three other men stood by whispering, though Fred couldn't hear what they were saying due to the overly loud music blaring from a radio.

Umbers turned to Fred and pointed to the scene with a flourish in the way a small child proudly points to their newest creation. "Well," he beamed, "what do you think?"

Fred mustered up the only words he could find. "Yeah...they're... good-looking guys..." The tension lifted only to be replaced with an awkwardness that left Fred grasping for conversation. Big Tiny had moved uncomfortably close to Fred and put one hand on his shoulder.

Introductions were made, and the filming continued. At some point, Umbers leaned over and whispered, "Maybe you want to be a film star and make some loops."

"Oh yeah, I'll think about it," Fred said with all the interest he could manage.

He did think about it, and the images made him lose sleep. Nearly a year in, the case was finally building momentum. In the coming weeks, Fred and Ron let on that they had a sudden windfall of cash but nowhere to invest the extra green. Umbers cut them in on a deal to buy one million tabs of LSD from his associate, Lance, or Lancie as Umbers called him.

ON THE NIGHT the big buy went down, Fred stuck a cigar in his pocket. If he lit it, that would be the cue to the backup agents that he'd actually seen the pills, and they could move in for the arrests. Lance showed up at the designated location, a parking lot near the Bowery, with three others including Big Tiny. One of the Special Agents who was in a hidden location doing surveillance noticed that a man walked over to one of the men, talked for a while, then walked away. The feds had expected about six guys to show up with the drugs, and someone determined that the man who walked off may have escaped the arrest. So unbeknownst to anyone standing in the parking lot near the Bowery, one of the surveillance teams went searching for that missing man at the same time Fred was opening the containers of LSD. The pills were in oversized plastic bags inside of several large red storage drums. Fred moved the pills around and shook the containers from side to side to ensure that there were actually pills in there and not a bunch of filler. Then he took the cigar from his pocket...

The arrest happened without incident, and there was a fake arrest of Skull Murphy to give him coverage. It was shortly after this that a Special Agent pulled Fred aside to give him an update on the missing man. "What missing man?"

The agent explained what had happened and how someone saw this mystery man get on a bus after talking with Lance. With red lights flashing and sirens wailing, a team of agents had chased the bus down until it pulled over. They'd taken the mystery guy from the bus, arrested, and questioned him.

"I was just, uh just asking for directions to the museum," he'd explained. "I was sitting on the bus hearing these sirens and thinking,

'This might be the most exciting night of my life! I'm gonna see a bad guy get arrested. All of a sudden...*I'm* the bad guy!'"

As light-hearted as that situation was, Fred's nerves were on fire from the culmination of a year-long investigation that had ended safely and successfully. Tonight was not over though. The containers had to be brought back and put in an evidence locker after they were weighed. Sure enough Lance and company had "whacked the package." There were only about half a million pills.

Guys who dealt drugs were, almost by definition, not the most ethical of businessmen to begin with. There was no honor among thieves on the grimy cement sidewalks that served as their storefronts. It was almost a given in big drug deals that the amount of product promised was much lower than what was actually delivered, so no one was surprised by this. One popular trick was to stuff maybe three one-ounce fishing tackle weights inside a kilo of heroin, thereby leaving about ninety percent of the pure heroin in the block. Those three ounces or so would be cut with filler in a ten to one ratio, which swelled the original three ounces into thirty and resulted in a couple thousand extra dollars in profit.

"We won't be going bowling tonight?" Felix asked, referring to the time that one resourceful dealer had placed a bowling ball in the middle of an enormous container of pills to add weight. What was a buyer going to do? And the dealer would always have an excuse as to how someone else was responsible for the low amount of drugs in the container.

———

THEY'D STOPPED this batch from reaching the streets, but for every dealer they took out, the monstrous drug trade grew two more heads. The agents suspected the tablets were being produced on the west coast in commercial tableting machines like the ones used by pharmaceutical companies, but they couldn't identify the manufacturers. It would have been icing on the cake if Umbers had flipped on his source, but he wouldn't.

While the arrest of Umbers did have a successful conclusion, the agents were never able to link him to the Colombo shooting. Fred was discouraged at this.

"Remember what your dad always said," Ginger reminded him at home. "Make sure you wake up every day and enjoy it more than the day before because…"

Fred nodded. "…one day you'll wake up and find out you're dead. And then you'll be dead for a long time."

THE ADRENALINE RUSH from last night was still dancing about Fred's brain when he awoke the next morning filled with a mixture of satisfaction and regret. Was there any point in doing all this work only to have it shut down by a federal prosecutor? This was something that happened with frustrating frequency due to laws and politics. Was the danger he put himself in worth it? In 1973 they'd been blessed with Suzie who was still a baby, and would she and Ginger cope if something happened to him? The situation added another page to the mental book in his head titled "Did I Make the Right Decision?" After college Fred had used his teaching degree to land a job in a high school as an English teacher where he was also a basketball coach. He loved the job but always had a fascination with TV shows such as *The FBI Story* with Jimmy Stewart and movies about 1930s criminals John Dillinger and Pretty Boy Floyd.

Throughout college he'd started to feel that he wanted to be the good guy in a real-life gangster drama. During his senior year of college in 1968, he and eight friends had called every government agency they could think of to request applications: the FBI, Secret Service, Customs, and more. But they'd all gotten the same news back; there was a hold on hiring, so most of the guys gave up and went on with plan B for their lives. Then out of the blue, Fred got a call back for a preliminary interview and test despite the hiring hold. He scored well and was filled with wild delight at the prospect of living a life of excitement. It was definitely what he wanted to do, and told them so at the interview.

"A lot of people think we're out there undercover and chasing people with guns, but the work is rather mundane," an interviewer told him point blank. "The Secret Service tails the president around all day, and the FBI follows up on stolen cars and draft dodgers. Sure, there's the occasional bank robbery, but it's on a very limited scale."

Fred's heart sunk. "I'll need to consider this," he said with disappointment. "In all honesty, I was picturing something a little more thrilling."

"Look kid, if you want excitement, you should go with the Bureau of Narcotics and Dangerous Drugs. They work on the Mob, international drug smugglers, street gangs, and whatnot. I'll be honest with you. It's not for the faint of heart. Sure there's excitement, but there's a lot of danger nearly every day."

Fred had never heard of the agency, but then again it had only been created in 1968. Then in 1973, this bureau was combined with some other government agencies to create the DEA.

"Look, there are some friends of mine at the FBI who are planning to transfer. It's a new branch, so there are great opportunities for promotions."

Fred had reservations. He had a steady job teaching high school. He could continue coaching basketball, a game he loved so much. Was it too dangerous for a family man?

He talked it over with Ginger; they made all their important decisions together. "If that's your dream, at least give it a try," she encouraged him earnestly. Nothing made her happier than seeing him fulfilled, and vice versa. So he applied, and eighteen months later signed on with the bureau. And from the start it *was* exciting. But then the travelling started, and he was away from his family for days or weeks at a time. The hours were unpredictable. And when he mixed in the threats, risks, and unsavory characters he dealt with on a daily basis, sometimes he wondered if it really was all worth it.

Today was one of those days. Instead of ushering a group of hormonal teenagers into class for a lesson on irony, Fred would be focusing on new drug stings—that is when he finally made it to work. His car crept along in heavy traffic that darted like masses of cockroaches scurrying then stopping, and he completed his mental checklist of questions to go through. He'd be meeting with one of his informants today: Vinny, "The Cat." The guy was an organized crime informant who claimed to be the nephew of famous mobster Lucky Luciano. But everything Luciano was as a gangster, Vinny was not. Luciano held the Mob's code of silence and honor, the *rule of omerta*, sacred while Vinny made his living selling street information to the feds.

Although Vinny was a socially high-level mob associate who was allowed into their operation, he was not a made man in any of the crime families. He dealt drugs for the Capos and soldiers, stole cars, and helped with other crimes. He'd somehow weaseled his way into the lower-level fabric of their organization, yet never became a confidante, due to him being so obviously untrustworthy. Still, it was always a battle for agents to get funding and manpower for their potential cases, and they had to prove the information in hand was stellar. There were 300–350 agents for all of New York State, which meant they were spread thin. Because of this, the DEA required that in order to expend manpower, the minimum amount from a supplier was 2,000 pounds of marijuana, 2 kilos of cocaine, or 1 kilo of pure heroin.

One of Fred's nicknames was "The Man with the Magic Pen." If the number of cases dwindled, which wasn't often, and his group came across an informant who knew someone who could get 300 pounds of marijuana, Fred would interview the informant and find out who this person was getting the 300 pounds from. This usually led back to Mr. Big who might be supplying 3,000 pounds. So, Fred would write that his provider's organization is capable of distributing 3,000 pounds on a regular basis. Along with this, being able to write a report that said the information came from Lucky's nephew Vinny helped give the situation credibility. It was a win-win for everyone.

CHAPTER
SIX

FLORIDA
January 23, 1977

IN THE THINNING LIGHT, the trees around the sinkhole loomed a dark shade of green, almost black. The Florida humidity intensified Ronnie Ray's inability to catch his breath. Shifting from foot to foot in the sandy soil, he finally leaned over with his hands on his knees and inhaled deeply. Steinhorst had a psychopathic ability to sense fear and disapproval, both emotions he considered weaknesses. And both emotions were coursing through Ronnie Ray. This nut who was still holding the gun wouldn't hesitate to put a bullet through anyone he sensed was rattled enough to go to the police. Even Hughes was uncharacteristically silent; it was obvious Steinhorst was out of his mind tonight.

Steinhorst's words barely registered in Ronnie Rays's brain. The psycho was continuing to verbally torment the two terrified girls until finally announcing, "Ok, kids. Your two minutes are almost up. Have you thought of anything you could do to save your lives?" Steinhorst yanked the gag off the first girl, and her words were unintelligible through the sobs.

"*No!* Just stop this." A shout rose louder than the crying girls. Glaring, Steinhorst approached Ronnie Ray—a look of death on his face—then he stopped suddenly. There was a kind of charged silence obtainable only when one person dares to challenge the other. Killing was a part of the drug business, one Ronnie Ray hoped he'd never witness, of course. But this went beyond business. He couldn't stand it any longer. His demeanor shriveled. "Steinhorst, no. This has gone far enough. Do what you gotta do, but don't keep this up. We need to get out of here." He'd blurted it out, and there was no taking it back.

Steinhorst, lips curled, stepped closer to Ronnie Ray and paused. With those cold eyes and blank stare boring into him, Ronnie Ray imagined the gun being leveled at his head. Unexpectedly, Steinhorst walked casually toward the teens and in quick succession, two bright flares of light exploded from the gun. In the brief muzzle flashes, the deadly scene tattooed itself into Ronnie Ray's memory, especially the girls' coats and blouses splattered with red. It was a horror he wouldn't shake for the rest of his life. Two beautiful young girls blown away.

Ronnie Ray felt sick in the midst of the total silence. Again, the strong smell of gunpowder lingered, and very slowly, he snapped out of his mind's foggy haze. Like the breaking of dawn. Gradually the quiet was broken by crickets chirping, and he caught sight of a scampering gecko near his feet.

"Just remember, you weak sons of bitches, it don't matter who pulled the trigger. Say one word about this, and I'll blow your head off!" Steinhorst was spitting mad. He brandished his pistol and pointed it between Hughes, Ronnie Ray, and the dead bodies near the sinkhole. "*It's murder for anyone involved, and in Florida that means the death penalty,*" he hissed.

Ronnie Ray's arms hung stiffly at his side; his tongue was so dry he couldn't swallow. He'd known Steinhorst for quite some time and had been witness to the horrors this man was capable of.

"Now we get rid of these bodies," Steinhorst said in an unconcerned tone. He was vacillating between uncontrollable fits of rage and moments of self-control.

For what seemed like hours, they worked to wrap each body with thick industrial electric wire, which they attached to heavy cinder blocks. They grunted, sweated, and strained to lug each victim into a small hunting boat, which they paddled to the middle of the lake before heaving the bodies overboard.

Ronnie Ray, Hughes, and Steinhorst burned their clothes and a mattress that had been in the van. Steinhorst was paranoid they'd forgotten to cover their tracks and threatened them all that there had better not be any loose ends. Throughout the coming weeks, Ronnie Ray couldn't wash his hands enough to scour away the death. He washed and washed and washed, but the feeling of blood seemed to remain.

While they were disposing of the bodies, the drugs were being delivered to a warehouse. The drive back was excruciatingly long. By the time Ronnie Ray returned to Panama City, he was sick with nausea.

WHEN RONNIE RAY finally collected his cash, he informed Steinhorst he was done. They were standing near a garage by a house where Steinhorst had directed him to meet up.

"I don't think I can do this anymore," he said, pocketing the wad of bills. The past day had been agonizing hell for Ronnie Ray, after seeing what the captives had gone through. He had a vision of the girls that he wished he could expunge from his brain. The uncontrollable shaking last night had left him with ice in his stomach.

"Those kids..."

Steinhorst glared with fists clenched at his side. "Ronnie Ray, do you even understand this business? Do you think I enjoyed doing what I had to do to protect you and everyone else?" As irrational as Steinhorst could be, even he was moved by Ronnie Ray's past attempts to draw those around him into a pathetic pseudo-family of misfits. He didn't coddle Ronnie Ray. He didn't seem capable of that much compassion. But occasionally he was patient with Ronnie Ray in a way he wasn't with others. But when Ronnie Ray didn't respond, the calmness in Steinhorst's voice evaporated as quickly as it had come; his face contorted back into the madman. "Do you damn well understand what I'm saying?" He jabbed a finger into Ronnie Ray's chest. "I will never," he was suddenly screaming, "*never* be locked up in a damn cage like an animal again! You're not done. You agreed to help with this deal, and the deal ain't over until the loads are put out!" He grabbed a shovel leaning against a nearby tree and heaved it angrily. "*I'll be calling you,*" he barked, then turned to his truck and got in, slamming the door behind him.

———

RONNIE RAY WENT through the next several days moody and sullen. Something inside of him had changed forever. He had watched a guy get blasted away in a pickup. The sickening pool of blood dripping off the seat wouldn't leave his head. And he couldn't stop reliving what the girls went through—shivering in the cold, lying there in blood-stained clothing. Executed. He turned off the news and refused to look at a newspaper. The continued press coverage about the four missing people threw him further into depression. The worst was when the missing sisters' parents appeared on the nightly news pleading for some word.

It felt as though it would only be a matter of days before the law came knocking on his door. They already had leads. When the crew had heard Steinhorst's gun go off, some of them had been out on the water and didn't know what happened. They assumed the whole deal had gone bad and left, and one group scuttled their boat. They'd left about thirty bales of marijuana floating in the water. Without their help, the other two crews couldn't get the whole load off the *Gunsmoke* before sunrise, so the cops found 3,000 pounds of marijuana just sitting on the shore along with one of the small boats used for ferrying. It was partly submerged, and Ronnie Ray heard word that it had already been traced back to that idiot Bobby Vines who owned all three of the fourteen-foot ferry boats. Then someone had steered the big shrimper west of Egmont Key and sunk the whole thing. Hughes had disappeared. *Yeah, it won't be long before they connect my name to the whole mess,* he thought.

Ronnie Ray waited with a lump in his throat for Steinhorst's call. But he wanted to be out of this business for good. Starting tomorrow, he'd look for a new honest job.

CHAPTER
SEVEN

FLORIDA/NEW JERSEY
Late January 1977

RONNIE RAY SHIFTED SLEEPILY beneath a twist of sheets. A relentless ringing from the next room broke through muffled shouts and doors banging in the yards around his trailer. He stirred from a late-afternoon nap and headed toward the phone in the next room, all the while dreading the thought of who might be on the other line. The gruff voice confirmed his worst fear.

"Be at the warehouse tomorrow night at 11:00. We have to get a run up the coast. Don't even think of being late. And don't piss me off." It was Steinhorst, and refusing the command would be as useful as telling the sun not to rise, but he gave it a shot.

"My son's sick. There ain't no one else to watch him," he lied.

"Look, Ronnie Ray, every business has some inconveniences. That doesn't mean you stop production or delivery. It's like the old saying 'the show must go on.' So I don't give two shits if you're watching Christ himself. Figure out your problem and *be there* or I'll see that you don't ever have to worry about 'watching' your son again."

Steinhorst hung up without so much as a "goodbye," leaving Ronnie Ray standing by the phone for several minutes trying to wrangle a way out of this web spun by an insane killer. It had been days since the murders, and this was the first time he'd heard from Steinhorst since that night—a memory that forced a sudden weight to settle in Ronnie Ray's stomach. Finally confronting his destiny caused a sickening gust of low mood to dwell within him. He vowed to stay clear, to get out of the business and forge his own path. But he was being pulled back in, like sinking in deadly quicksand.

He walked into the bathroom to splash water on his face and saw in the mirror that his sunken eyes were now darkly rimmed. He knew too much. *If I don't show tomorrow, I'll be the next one to have a bullet in me.* Or worse, my son. Steinhorst was not only his boss but was ruthless. And crazy enough to keep anyone who worked under him from stepping out of line. Everyone followed Steinhorst's orders as though they were political prisoners, not daring to question or deviate.

He pondered how money does strange things to people. The cash had been so good and easy that he'd been hooked after the first deal, and for a long time the risk had been worth the easy green. Ronnie Ray had bought a new dually truck and put a sizeable down payment on a small ranch house. Not bad for a guy who left school in the eighth grade and had already served two short terms in a state prison for burglary and armed robbery. Having nice clothes for his son and a roof over his head were priorities, not just an excuse to keep bringing in wads of cash. For this four-day run, he would get $5,000—more than he'd make working at the local mill for two months.

He promised himself there wouldn't be any more runs after this though. His wife was always concerned, mostly because their only son was twelve, and it wouldn't be fair to him if Ronnie Ray wound up dead or in prison. If only he hadn't agreed to unload that damn shrimp boat the night of the murders.

He was still shaken emotionally by the murders (he pictured the two teenage girls so full of life one moment then taken away to be murdered) that it kept him from sleeping at night. His conscience jerked him awake every time he came close to nodding off. His body was dulled by the lingering exhaustion, he couldn't concentrate—had Steinhorst said 11:00 or 12:00?—and he was irritable. Irritable at Steinhorst for yanking his strings as though he were no more than a puppet, and irritable that he'd even accepted this last job. He couldn't shake the feeling that he was never meant to show up at the shrimp boat that fateful night, but he'd gone and charted his own course instead of following what karma meant for him to do. There was no going back now.

⊏⊐

THE NEXT EVENING, Ronnie Ray stood beneath a dark sky filled with thick, ragged clouds that carried with them a threat of approaching storms. Steinhorst had a temperature-controlled tractor trailer waiting along with a few grunt workers to help move bundles. Clear through the night, they loaded the trailer with sixty-pound bales of marijuana as fast as possible until their shirts were soaked in perspiration. Ronnie Ray's eyes ached with sleeplessness, and when the crashes of thunder started building outside, it echoed the storminess of his own life. He counted down the hours until this last job would be over. The first step was over; the trailer was loaded, and he climbed into the cab. Everything had gone fine. He convinced himself he was just jittery from focusing too much on this being his last job and thinking that carried some kind of bad omen; it seemed something always happened to keep him down.

"Be smart, Ronnie Ray," Steinhorst was telling him through the rolled-down window. Follow the speed limit. If you plan on racing to New Jersey, you might as well just turn yourself in to the cops now. Gas up at the pumps farthest away from the building so people can't smell the pot. And if you pull over to sleep, pull into a designated area, not some suspicious side road." He warned Ronnie Ray that they couldn't afford another "misstep" like the other night. He referred to unexpectedly killing four people as if he were guilty of a minor engineering flaw at an automotive plant and now had to send out a little card reminding people to get it fixed in less than an hour at their friendly neighborhood dealer. "Listen, it's no big deal. Just try to forget it. Shit happens, and we didn't have a choice. Remember, it doesn't matter who pulled the trigger. We're all guilty."

Ronnie Ray nodded and with heavy eyelids took the slip of paper he was handed.

———

THE TRACTOR TRAILER loaded with 15,000 pounds of marijuana rolled through small town after small town, and the rural countryside was teeming with towering red oak and birch trees. Ronnie Ray could have enjoyed the scenery, but he was straining to stay awake, and also focus on the ever-changing speed limits. His mind whirled with thoughts of the two teenage girls. Were their friends looking for them? Did their families hold out hope that the girls had run away and would return soon? Worst of all, what if the families never learned the fate of the four innocent victims?

In spite of the AC running, a bead of sweat dripped from his brow, and his hands shook uncontrollably on the steering wheel. He was counting down the hours—thirty—until this last run was over. His nerves had never failed him this badly before; he needed to find a real job.

He'd only dared to pull over and sleep for a few hours outside of High Point, North Carolina. He was no longer capable of real sleep but rather a terrifying state of semi-consciousness that pulled him deeper into a panicked state of crippling anxiety.

Suddenly, far down the highway, flashing red lights appeared on the horizon. Ronnie Ray's heart seized, and out of instinct his foot went to the brake, but there was nowhere for him to turn off on the two-lane road. He swore and pounded his hands on the steering wheel. Sweat broke out on his brow, and when he traveled half a mile farther, he found a line of traffic had come to a halt. That familiar sense of powerlessness washed over him, and his fingers started trembling violently.

At the end of the snaking line he could make out two cars that had apparently been in an accident. Two police officers were standing on the road next to them and the crescendo of an ambulance siren wailed in the distance. From his perch above the cars, he could see the action play out. While he was relieved on one hand, a bout of paranoia settled in. He worried one of the police had a drug dog with him, and perhaps the wind was blowing that direction. Why had he pulled so close to the other cars? He felt as though he were suffocating. He rolled down a window and stuck his hand out like a weather vane. It was the first good sign he'd had in weeks, there was a fortunate cross breeze. Still, each minute dragged on until the police cleared one side of the road and started letting traffic through. When it was finally his turn, he let the car in front of him have a head start so he could pass the cops without having to slow down. It was a plan that almost worked. The policeman directing traffic stopped the line two cars ahead of Ronnie Ray and let the other side through.

An officer sweeping up some glass stopped midstep and froze. He looked around, and Ronnie Ray was certain he was sniffing the air. *God, please let that breeze blow the smell away from them* he prayed for what may have been the first time in his life. Then, before the cop had time to act, the line of cars was moving again, and Ronnie Ray passed without detection. He drove five more miles down the road, pulled over to the side, got out, and threw up. By the time his heart had stopped pounding, he realized he was near his destination and quickly sought out a telephone booth at the edge of a small New Jersey town.

The voice on the other end paused before saying, "Yeah?"

"Is this Katko?" Ronnie Ray asked. In spite of the area being virtually deserted, he looked around to ensure no one could overhear. Had anyone seen him, he'd have certainly appeared to be suspiciously hiding something.

"Who wants to know? Who's this?"

"I've got a delivery from Florida." A white car trolled by, and Ronnie Ray stiffened, certain it was an unmarked cop car coming to arrest him, but the car passed by.

"Great. I'll be waiting." The line went dead.

Ronnie Ray had been informed that Katko was a high-level contact for all of the East Coast deliveries. He owned an oil and gas business that had been struggling financially about a year ago, and at the same time, he'd been propping up a money-guzzling horse farm as well. To get away from his troubles, he went to a horse show where he'd connected with a Texas associate and jumped at the chance to distribute marijuana in return for enough money to keep his business going awhile longer.

Ronnie Ray pulled into a long drive on the rural property and saw Katko waiting as he said he'd do. He motioned for Ronnie Ray to follow behind him in the tractor trailer.

"I'll show you where to back her up," he shouted from a distance. Up ahead stood a weather-worn horse barn with its double doors swung wide open. Ronnie Ray backed the vehicle into the entrance of the barn and killed the motor. With the help of some workers, they labored feverishly to unload the tons of marijuana, with each bale removed being a load off of Ronnie Ray's mind as well. The finish line was within sight. Just before dark the trailer lay empty, and the two men headed into the ranch-style house.

After some coffee and casual conversation, Ronnie Ray realized Katko wasn't a professional drug dealer. He lacked the typical paranoia and surliness. Katko was middle-aged and had almost immediately revealed that he'd only started dealing to produce much-needed cash during the slow summer season. "Hell," he shrugged, "it's a harmless drug. No one's ever been hurt smoking a joint."

Near the kitchen was a row of trophies topped with shiny gold or silver horses. It was due to his horses that Katko had first met a guy named Raymond Hawkins. There was nothing about Hawkins, this young entrepreneur, that indicated he'd already been convicted of drug charges. One rainy Saturday, the two had bumped into each other at a horse show. They quickly bonded while talking the day away. Katko had revealed to Hawkins that he was looking at selling a horse due to a cash flow problem. Though Katko and Hawkins hit it off with their love of horses, their conversation shifted to getting rich. Although Katko initially rejected the idea, he was quickly absorbed into the "harmless" business of wholesale distribution of marijuana—due to Katko's location, access to horse trailers to move the bales, and having barns to store big loads.

In the kitchen, Katko produced three bundles of cash. It would have taken hours for Ronnie Ray to count it all, so instead the bundles were placed on a precision scale that weighed down to the milligram.

"This bundle is all Benjamins." Katko performed a quick flick through the bundles for Ronnie Ray's approval and placed them on the scale. "Three pounds at $45,400 per pound…" He punched buttons on a calculator and scribbled down a figure then removed the hundreds. "Some Grants…" He waited for the dial to stop twitching and wrote down more numbers. Ronnie Ray flipped through each bundle of bills the way Steinhorst had instructed him, and Katko showed no offense. *Trust no one* was everyone's motto in this business. He finished with some bundles of Jacksons, added the total and returned the slip of paper to Ronnie Ray saying, "You're in a good place, hauling the big loads and only dealing with me. No one else."

It was common knowledge that you deal with one person and your risk of getting caught is miniscule. Katko would sell the load in one- or two-thousand-pound increments, meaning his risk for getting caught and ripped off increased with each sale. Yet, he could still distribute it quickly, and in the world of large-scale distribution, that was essential. From there it would be divided into smaller amounts until some desperate soul took to dealing ounces to dozens of people, one of whom would surely end up getting pinched by the law and giving up the desperate soul's name in exchange for a slap on the wrist.

"This business is actually one of the best things that's ever happened to me, and I owe a lot to Steinhorst. Good guy. A little crazy, but a good guy," Katko commented.

"Yeah," Ronnie Ray replied flatly. He didn't bother to mention that the good guy was just crazy enough to have executed four innocent people.

When they were done, he found a motel about ten miles away and slept somewhat peacefully for the first time in over a week, but wouldn't be completely at ease until he was on his way back to Florida with a load of greenbacks and an empty trailer.

CHAPTER
EIGHT

NEW YORK
March 1977

WHEN FRED ARRIVED at DEA's New York office late that March morning, the first message he saw was from Vinny, "The Cat," the DEA paid informant Fred had worked with for most of his career. He had watched Vinny make a grand living, most of it from giving the feds information about some minor "drug lord" he met while hanging out in a shithole bar in Queens or Brooklyn. The problem with Vinny, besides being someone Fred considered the slimiest of scammers, was that his information was rarely what the government thought it would be. Vinny walked away with handfuls of cash, and the feds sat looking like defenseless children who'd been shaken down for their lunch money.

Most of the time, the "big information" Vinny boasted about was just some little wannabe bragging about all of his supposed drug connections. Vinny would seize the opportunity and tell the chump that he had people with enormous sums of money who were desperate to find new drug suppliers. After that, it was always the same simple game plan. Vinny would introduce the chump to the money man, one of DEA's undercover agents posing as a Mafia wise guy. Sometimes the

Special Agent posed as a prosperous businessman interested in buying cocaine for his Wall Street friends. It didn't matter. The sellers only felt the dollar signs popping out of their eyes, and Vinny would direct the show from there. After a few meetings, everyone would feel comfortable, and Vinny would vanish. The agent would continue negotiating, much the way any buyer negotiates for a legal commodity. Once the price and terms of delivery were agreed upon, a few small buys would take place to build trust. Finally, a big quantity would be ordered, and that's when the chump would be arrested.

If all went as expected; some of the chump's associates would be identified through surveillance, undercover conversations, telephone recordings, and other investigative efforts. The DEA had a parking lot full of undercover vehicles such as gas or telephone trucks, complete with matching uniforms to help disguise their stakeouts. Again, it didn't matter. In every case, the chump would be given the chance to cooperate. He usually did, and when there was enough evidence, the others in the case would be arrested. The agents never really wanted the chump to begin with; they were going after The Big One. Over and over and over. Though not sophisticated, it was very effective.

The problem with Vinny was that in his mind, he elevated every loser he met into some big shot drug lord. Vinny would tell the DEA he knew a Mr. Big who could supply five kilos of heroin on a regular basis. In the end, it would be half a kilo, and Vinny would clasp his head in shock saying, "What? I could swear he was gonna come up with the whole amount!" But the agents always nabbed Mr. Big for just enough to make it worthwhile and to keep chasing Vinny's leads.

In spite of claiming to be related to Lucky Luciano, Vinny couldn't hold a candle to the famous gangster. Vinny was a small-timer, and his cases never led to anything of any consequence. The people he set up were low-level dirtbags who never got any closer to major drug suppliers than most high school basketball players get to the NBA. It was just one low-life after another, and all of them hoping to make the big score that would lift them to the next level. Amazingly, they even looked the same and lived in the same seedy neighborhoods. To survive, they would buy a small quantity of cocaine, cut it, and then snort it up their noses before they could make a profit. Their only big payday came after they met Vinny. He always had customers lining up to pay top dollar for the same adulterated shit that couldn't be given away on the street.

For reasons that were hard to figure out, the DEA bosses in New York never saw a problem with the petty suppliers Vinny set up to get busted. Vinny's people were nickel-and-dime street dealers. Maybe the supervisors didn't see a problem because Vinny, like most of the DEA's informants, served a number of purposes that were instrumental in being able to continue the war on drugs. Most importantly, Vinny's setups added to the office's arrest and seizure statistics. This was all part of a game that each office was forced to play in a never-ending battle for more manpower and funding. If the New York office didn't produce the statistics, another office would. There was only enough money funneling in for some of the offices to grow; big offices led to more people available to do more work. As absurd as it was, the more people in an office, the more funding they received for raises, along with new carpeting and plusher furniture. So it was bigger paychecks and more prestige that caused many of the bosses to love punks like Vinny.

Fred detested informants like Vinny, but guys like him were needed. Vinny was as deceitful as a demon and wore his trickery like a crown. He bragged about once helping his own mother kill his father's girlfriend. But like most of his claims, this one rang hollow. Fred got a certain amount of enjoyment whenever he heard that Vinny, The Cat, had used up another of his nine lives during some altercation with one of the people he set up. After surviving five shootings and two stabbings, Vinny didn't seem to have much time left. Knowing that The Cat would be calling with yet another fabulous tale about some major drug cartel figure with a hundred kilos of cocaine, Fred tossed aside the message he'd gotten when he first walked in. He'd reach out to The Cat on his time.

Fred again ignored the ringing phone on his desk. It was 11:00 a.m., and he had weekly reports to finish. Whoever it was that kept calling every few minutes could wait or call 9-1-1 if it was that much of an emergency. As team leader, Fred had extra duties without extra time to finish them. Besides reports, he had to collect mileage totals, approve leave, and finish other mundane tasks. "You're a different breed," Fred's partner told him on more than one occasion when Fred made it clear he'd never allow himself to be promoted above the level of a group supervisor. Anything higher and he would just become another administrator. Other Special Agents would tell Fred, "Everyone in this office is gunning for you to be the boss. You're fair and honest and organized." But he didn't want to be stuck at a desk. It was his love of the streets and landing arrests that fueled him on. "Make every day better than the one before," was his dad's mantra and a saying Fred lived by.

When the phone started ringing again after only a ten-second lapse, he finally gave in. "Special Agent Fred Boff," he said brusquely, hoping to convey his impatience with what was likely to be a time-wasting conversation.

"Fred, what's up?"

He knew by the high-pitched, ear-piercing shrill that it was Vinny, someone who surely couldn't care less that Fred was extremely busy.

Fred winced and pulled the phone a few inches from his ear. "What do you need, Vinny?" Vinny always needed something.

"Got a problem, my man. I don't have a way to get to the park. Did you hear me, Fred? I got a problem. I don't have a way to get to the park. Can you come by my place and get me?"

Out of all of Vinny's annoying traits—and there were many—his disturbing tendency to repeat everything he said topped the list. Fred racked his brain but couldn't remember talking with Vinny about "the park." Fred always arranged out-of-the-way secluded places to meet his informants to protect both of them from being recognized. But he had no plans to meet up with Vinny right now.

Fred sighed in exasperation. "Vinny, it seems like you always have a problem. But why would I meet you in the park now when I'm finishing paperwork?"

"This is urgent. Like 'right now' information. It's big. Really big, but you gotta hurry. It'll be worth it. You have my word. It's urgent. Like 'right now,'" Vinny promised, suave-voiced as always but talking much faster than he normally did. "But I don't have my car. You need to pick me up."

"Are you kidding? You never owned a car. Anything you've ever driven was someone else's car. Some poor sucker who forgot and left the keys in the ignition for a minute."

"Fred, that's not true. I haven't stolen a car since I started working for you guys."

That was doubtful, but Vinny had a need to control every conversation. "Give me a break. Hatch and I will be by in an hour and pick you up at the bridge near your place. We'll be in a blue Lincoln." Fred's partner, Everett "Hatch" Hatcher, strolled into the room and heard the tail end of the conversation. Fred, who was very tall, talkative, and quick to bend the rules stood in stark contrast to Hatch who was black, stocky, and went through life with a military-level fondness for rules. They were one of the first multiracial agent teams and soon became the new *Odd Couple* at the office. Their differences made them a strong team as well as a believable couple.

"You're driving a Lincoln now? Boy, being a fed must really pay well."

"It doesn't pay that well. We're just lucky there are so many fine Americans like you out there who keep dealing shit to kids. That way we can seize their cars."

"Fred, one other thing. As a favor to me, can you bring somebody other than Hatch? You know…a black dude with a gun… It makes me nervous. As a favor to me."

"Screw you, Vinny. You'll never run into a better person to deal with than Hatch. And you better have some damn good info, and don't be late. One hour." Fred hung up the phone.

Hatch just shook his head at Vinny's last remark.

Though known for his fairness and deserved compassion, Fred had little use for corrupt and insincere informants like Vinny. "Don't let a piece of shit like him bother you, Hatch," Fred responded. "Anyway, what people should be worried about is guys like Vinny with a gun. That's what makes me nervous."

Hatch shook off the comment and laughed. "Remember that time in Georgia?"

Fred looked up from the note he was writing regarding Vinny. "The time we went to the café with a white section and black section?"

48

"You got it. That waitress who looked like she hadn't taken a bath in a month brought you a glass of water and a menu and ignored me."

Fred nodded. "Then she came, turned her back to you, and took my order, leaving you sitting there with your mouth open and your stomach growling. Then you asked me, 'Fred, you're my friend, right?'"

"To which you sarcastically replied, 'Most of the time, unless you piss me off.'"

"Then you asked, 'Is it possible that I'm black?' and I unfortunately had to inform you that it was probably because you're a smart-ass Special Agent and she could sense it." Fred slapped his desk and chuckled, recalling how Hatch had turned the situation humorous.

After that they walked to the elevator, giving a just-so-you-know-we're-leaving-now wave to the secretaries on their way out. "Then you told me, 'You're a pretty smart guy. That's a great observation! I think you *are* black."

"Then we got up and walked out of that redneck joint. We had to get bags of chips and candy bars at the gas station. We truly are the odd couple," Fred grinned.

They were an odd match but became a great team nonetheless. A former major in the army, Hatch possessed the burliness and confidence of someone who had accomplished so much in life that it didn't occur to him to waste time worrying about a derogatory comment spilling from the mouth of scum like Vinny. Hatch had the ability to find the humor in any situation, and was sharp witted enough to come up with jokes and pranks on the fly.

He was made of strong stuff. As a black man married to a white woman in the 1970s, he had to be. He did what was right and didn't care if others didn't see it the same way. He once answered his own front door to find a salesman. The man was clearly surprised to see a black man in what was obviously an all-white neighborhood. "Uh… are you the, uh… Is the owner of the home here?"

Hatch just shook his head. He was used to people making assumptions about him.

There'd been more than one occasion over the years when Fred and Hatch found themselves alone in an interview room with some low-life drug dealer who invoked the "n word." The first time it happened, Fred stood up and poked his finger right in the loser's face. "Let me hear you use that filthy word again…"

Hatch had just patted Fred's arm and with no emotion simply said, "Settle down partner and consider the source."

His even tone, which implied the drug dealer was so despicable as to be inconsequential, had come across as more of an insult than any words could have. Fred's intensity was often balanced by Hatch who strolled through life with a peaceful and carefree faith.

As they rounded a corner, a man came stumbling from between two cars into their path and Fred hit the brakes. The man shook a fist at them and yelled something vulgar, revealing a mouth that beheld only a few teeth.

"That man's mouth gave me another flashback to Georgia," Fred said and let out a low whistle of relief at the near miss.

"The motel?" Hatch chuckled and Fred nodded. "But I'm quite certain that the man at the motel had only one tooth."

It had been late at night after a long and frustrating interview in a small Georgia town with only one rundown motel advertising *Vacancy* on its neon sign.

"The wall-sized stars-and-bars rebel flag behind the check-in counter should have been our first clue," Fred said pointedly. "The way that scrawny night manager leaned back in his chair, chewing on a plastic straw and looking back and forth from you to me as though he were deciding our entire fate…"

"Maybe he just thought we were cute!"

"Nope. Not a chance. And then he had the balls to triumphantly announce that he would not rent us a room."

"I stood there cool as a cucumber. You're the one who went ballistic and," Hatch stopped to laugh aloud, "and *you* threatened him!"

"It wiped that smug grin right off his face."

"We're federal agents! You'll rent us a room, damn it, or I'll take it!" Hatch said imitating Fred the best he could.

"We got the room, and then I regretted it. First thing I did was put my gun under the pillow." Fred referenced how Hatch had placed his handgun across the room on a table. "'What the hell are you doing?' I asked you, and you told me to relax."

"You should have relaxed. It was all good, but you got all riled up thinking the guy was from the Ku Klux Klan or something."

"He probably was. I told you some of the guys in that town ran around with white sheets over their heads at night. Hell, that manager could have been the leader. But five minutes after we lay down, you were snoring. I was up until midnight growing an ulcer and jumping at every sound. I had the image of us being hanged from a tree right outside of our motel room."

"And who ended up being right?" Hatch said with another satisfied chuckle.

DURING THE TWENTY minutes it took to get to Vinny's place near the Brooklyn Bridge, Hatch cracked some jokes about Vinny. With a bit of time to spare, they stopped and bought a few dirty water dogs and two sodas. Hatch ate his hesitantly at first, but Fred had such an affinity for hot dogs that the thought of eating one, even from a street cart, didn't faze him. Fred lived by a lot of personal rules, not the least of which was that you had to buy the hot dogs from street vendors early in the day. That way, there was a chance, though not much of one, that the water was still clean. Some of the vendors never changed the water, but as with everything in life, he considered this slight chance better than none at all.

They drove around to the park side of the bridge before tearing into the rest of the hot dogs. To Fred's surprise, Vinny was on time, as they pulled up. There he stood, all five-and-a-half feet of him and thin as a needle. Fred hoped Vinny wouldn't smile, but he did. The edges of his mouth turned upward into a forced grimace that resulted in a revolting Grinch-type grin. It was irritating to look at.

Vinny climbed in, and as they drove to a parking lot he griped in his weasely voice, "Aaah. I see you didn't bring me a dog. I guess I'm not that important. I'm just your damn stool. I said I'm not that important, I'm just your damn stool, right?"

Fred turned to the backseat and gave Vinny a hard stare before taking a bite of his hot dog. He chewed slowly and deliberately while watching Vinny grow impatient. Finally he said, "Okay, Vinny. You're right. You're just a stool. You'd sell your own mother for a few bucks if you had the chance." His voice implied he didn't have time for these games, and he refused to play into Vinny's ploy for sympathy, getting right to the point instead. "Vinny, we're done paying for crap information. Don't give me anymore low-level losers. You've gotten some good money for bad info, and this needs to be good. So far you haven't impressed me."

Vinny raised his arms like a television evangelist does just before shamelessly pleading with the audience to send money. But this plea was different. "You can trust me. Honest. You can trust me."

Fred pulled into a semi-vacant parking lot and killed the engine. It was a relatively deserted area except for a group of teenagers milling around on a corner, necks craning as they peered up and down the street like meerkats on the savannah.

"This is good, good, good stuff involving thousands of pounds of pot, shipments from boats coming in, airplanes, drug runs all over the place. It's a big one, maybe the biggest bust of your whole career." Vinny paused for dramatic effect before confidently adding, "And I'll need five hundred thousand for the info." And then to Fred's dismay, he repeated himself.

Hatch shook his head and Fred burst out laughing. "You're kidding me, right? There's no way the department will approve a half-million-dollar payoff, Vinny. If you want like five thousand dollars, let's hear what you can do."

Vinny fidgeted, rolling the end of his cigarette between thumb and index finger, frustrated at Fred dropping two zeroes from the dollar amount. He let out a long sigh. "All right. My guy from Queens is a middleman who buys big loads of pot from a guy in Jersey. The Jersey guy is sitting on twenty-five, maybe fifty tons *right now*. The Jersey guy's name is Katko, and his big scores come in from Florida on boats out of Colombia, but I think the top people are in Tennessee, Georgia, and Texas. My middleman said the driver out of Florida mentioned a big shot involved, with the last name of Hawkins. I think he said the dude was from down south, but they're all connected to it." He took a long drag on a cigarette and blew out a long stream of smoke before adding all the details he knew about the supposed cartel. He was reveling in being the one in-the-know about a big drug deal.

"What else?" Fred asked, unimpressed by the information he'd heard so many times before. "We need names, locations, things like that. You've been around, Vinny. Don't play games."

"Yeah, yeah. Katko's name is Charles or William or something like that. One of those real royal names. Charles or William, a real royal name. He owns a horse farm and supposedly has the product delivered to him in eighteen wheelers and horse trailers. He gets 'em from his horse farm, ya' know, eighteen wheelers and horse trailers. My Queens partner can set this Katko up for a big buy giving you the chance to arrest him." He stuck the cigarette between his lips and displayed both hands like an open book to indicate he was handing this to Fred and Hatch on a silver platter.

"Keep talking, Vinny. You almost have my interest."

"Only problem is this guy's minimum order is a thousand pounds at four hundred per. A thousand pounds at four hundred per."

But they had heard this line from Vinny before. "Okay. I'll check some things out myself and get back to you in a week. But we're definitely not buying a thousand pounds; we'll seize the load, and if it turns out to be as big as you say, I might get you five to six thousand for your efforts," Fred replied, starting up the car again. Vinny had decided to walk back home.

"I know you'll do right by me, Fred. I trust you." He sat looking at Fred, door open and one leg already on the ground before pausing to ask, "One last thing: can you get me a 400k flash roll?"

"Vinny, you set it up. I'll take care of the rest. Remember, you may think you're a Special Agent, but you're just a stool. We'll handle the flash roll. Call me when you have a meeting arranged, and make sure we have some lead time." Fred shook his head. Only Vinny would think Fred could sign out $400,000 from the DEA and then hand it over to Vinny to flash in front of Katko as proof that there was cash to pay for the drugs.

It sounded too good to be information Vinny would be privy to.

Likely he'd exaggerated every detail, as usual. Fred operated from the standpoint of assuming that every word spurting from Vinny's mouth was a lie until proven otherwise. Yet, something about this information was different than Vinny's usual blather. He'd look into it tomorrow. Tonight he had a party to attend in Greenwich Village and some sparkly pants Ginger was dying to see him wear. Although Ginger was eight months pregnant and busy with four-year-old Suzie at home, she was supportive of Fred's late nights and irregular hours. He was concerned with how much he'd be able to help her once the new baby was born. Would he have to cut back on work? How could he? His group was juggling not only another Greenwich Village case, but ten other investigations as well. When one wrapped up, three more would be waiting.

And when he got back to the office, his boss wanted a written report from Fred and Hatch ASAP. Hatch stayed up late that night, after helping his wife around the house, and finished and proofed his section of the report. Fred scribbled some minimal notes the next morning and handed it in along with Hatch's carefully detailed informational paperwork. Fred's report would get kicked back to be rewritten, but at least it would give him another week to get it done.

CHAPTER NINE

NEW YORK
March 1977

BAD INFORMATION and weak drug busts didn't sit well with the bosses in the long run. Fred had to get on top of Vinny's skewed information, double-check, and cross reference. He could count on at least part of every stool's information being false, a half-truth, or even completely fabricated. They wouldn't hesitate to double-cross a fed in a heartbeat.

Using Vinny's information, the paperwork was started as a Class 1 marijuana case. In the remarks, Fred wrote: **A reliable informant has reported that Charles Katko is a member of an international smuggling organization, capable of importing and distributing hundreds of thousands of pounds of marijuana each year**.

With this, they could open the case and use the information to justify hundreds of thousands of dollars for a flash roll that Katko would be shown as the buy money. Then Fred set about assigning the rest of the Special Agents in his group a job such as getting information on Katko's farm or setting up surveillance. Next he needed to pick an undercover agent. "I want Frank Marino for the UC. He's our best, and this is a big case." Fred had Hatch work on that.

Fred was running low on sleep, and his temples throbbed, partly from hunger. He hadn't eaten in hours. Last night's party at one of their usual Greenwich gay bars hadn't danced itself out until two in the morning. When he'd finally arrived home, removed his makeup, and crawled into bed, Ginger had stirred and thanked him for coming home alive yet one more time.

"Alive but humiliated," Fred had replied. "That same guy keeps patting and pinching my butt. He rubs up against me and breaths on my neck. He appears out of nowhere, and all of a sudden…"

"Hmmm, good. Now you know what it's like to be a woman and get sexually harassed." Even when practically asleep, her wit was sharp.

"Yeah, but he pinches *hard*," Fred replied, still angling for sympathy.

"I know," Ginger whispered as she slowly drifted back to sleep.

Now Fred found himself wishing that he could squeeze in even a short nap, although he'd never consider doing something so unprofessional in the office. Then Hatch knocked on the door and suggested they go out for a bite, so the two headed down the street to a favorite deli. Hatch chose a bowl of Manhattan clam chowder. "Hot dog, everything on it—and I mean *everything* you've got that can possibly go on it —side of fries too." Fred, hot dog addict that he was, had repeated the same order countless times over the years. Out of habit he scanned the interior of the deli and noticed a cook wearing a grease-splotched apron who resembled someone Fred had seen at a gay bar in the Village.

A noon crowd swelled through the door and among them was Dick, an obnoxious Special Agent from their building. Upon seeing him, Fred and Hatch moved wordlessly from the counter to a table in the corner. Fred found the distinct pickling smell unique to delis either repulsive or appetizing, depending on how much alcohol he'd had the previous night. Currently, he was more focused on Dick than the smell and didn't want to miss out on hearing the agent put in his usual order, two mugs of hot water which, to the deli's credit, they always provided to him for a nominal fee.

Fred spoke to Hatch as he watched Dick accept the two steaming mugs. "I've been checking on this Katko from Jersey. He's clean with only some traffic violations, and the guy owns a legitimate fuel oil business as well as land outside New Brunswick." He paused when the cook emerged from the back and eyed Fred suspiciously while speaking briefly with a customer. Fred responded by looking at the cook rather than turning away, wondering if the man remembered him from the gay night club. Being recognized when not undercover was a persistent fear, yet there was nothing about the pair sitting in a diner that would lead anyone to think they were feds, so he continued talking quietly when the cook walked off. "The assessor confirmed land owned by Katko is listed as a farm, which qualifies for a tax break on the property. His record is really clean. The only problem he's ever had was a speeding ticket ten years ago, and to make it worse, he beat the ticket in court."

Both Fred and Hatch paused to watch Special Agent Dick take a tea packet out of his pocket and dunk it in one of the hot water mugs. Then they turned back to each other.

"This guy Katko doesn't sound like a drug dealer," Hatch commented.

They paused again and watched as Dick took several ketchup packets out of his pocket and squeezed them into the other mug. "I've never known anyone but Dick to consider that concoction to be tomato soup. He sure is a cheapskate," Hatch commented. At the counter, Dick stirred the tomato-tainted water and began sipping his odd soup.

"Like I said, he doesn't sound like a drug dealer," Hatch repeated, and in his typical analytical way took several minutes to relay to Fred how he'd considered the situation from every angle and wasn't hopeful there was any truth to it. But then, what did they expect? Vinny's information had never been reliable for any big busts.

After leaving the diner, Hatch stopped to buy a can of soda. He needed caffeine for the afternoon after a week of working long hours.

"Receipt?" the cashier asked.

"Yes, please," Hatch responded.

The cash register was out of paper, and the cashier fumbled with first finding a replacement roll and then meticulously getting the end threaded through the machine on multiple failed attempts while Fred shifted from foot to foot. "Sorry, I'm new at this," she explained.

"Let's go," Fred said, already halfway out the door.

Hatch motioned to the register.

"It's a twenty-cent receipt!" Fred moaned.

Hatch stood motionless waiting patiently for the receipt. "I keep track of all my expenses. And you *gotta* relax."

"If you added up the time we spent on your piddly receipts..." Fred started, but by then the cash register had hummed to life and was spitting out Hatch's slip of paper, which he filed carefully in the receipt section of his wallet.

They took the long way back to the office past the CBS Broadcast Center, Pat's Bar, and parking garages weighted with commuter cars. Two pigeons fluttered to the ground up ahead and started pecking at a piece of hot dog bun wedged in a crevice between the sidewalk and building. Fred reveled in the energy he absorbed from these streets that were part of birthing a nation. Over the hum of traffic, he complained throughout their walk back about the amount of paperwork waiting for him and how Hatch had slowed them down waiting for that damn twenty-cent receipt. He'd had the names Vinny gave them run through NADDIS—The Narcotics and Dangerous Drugs Information System— which was run by the DEA, to see if they got any hits on the system. Suddenly, Fred stopped. He felt cold liquid soaking his rear end.

He craned his neck trying to see his own backside and wiped his pant seat with one hand. "What the hell?" he asked Hatch who was hunched over in fits of laughter having just poured the remainder of his soda down the back of Fred's pants. "You son of a bitch! Now I'll be sticky all day. Why did you do that?"

"Maybe your ass will get stuck to the chair, and you can get some paperwork done."

An hour later, Fred could still hear Hatch occasionally breaking into laughter from down the hall.

CHAPTER
TEN

NEW YORK
Late 1970s

"YOU LYING PRICK! You're gonna get it!" The angry defendant jumped to his feet, sending his chair skidding across the floor on its side.

There were gasps from the observers in the courtroom, and then someone screamed, "He has a knife!"

The man glowered at the prosecutor who for the past ten minutes had listed a litany of reasons why the now irate defendant should be incarcerated in a federal prison. Without warning, the man charged, knife held shoulder level and ready for impalement. Panic ensued. The prosecutor bounded out of the way while at the same time the U.S. Marshal ran toward the threat.

Suddenly, a piercing *crack* could be heard above the commotion, and the defendant's legs turned to rubber beneath him. With a grunt, he collapsed to the floor in a limp heap, while his knife clattered onto the shiny white tile. Crazy Harry had come to the rescue again.

It was Assistant U.S. Attorney Harry Batchelder, Jr., or "Crazy Harry," as he was referred to by the Special Agents who knew him. Harry had been in the courtroom when the knife-toting defendant spiraled out of control. It was the second time Crazy Harry had punched out a defendant to protect those in the courtroom. This had earned respect for the large powerful ex-military man who was now an Assistant U.S. Attorney—a position more closely associated with dignity and self-control than cleaning someone's clock. Harry was a three-time decorated fighter pilot in Vietnam, which secured him the honor of being a hero, albeit one described by his military friends as "unique."

Fred had worked with him in the past and now prepared his notes for a call to Crazy Harry for some legal advice regarding how to proceed with what was shaping up to be some big drug busts. He wanted to make sure his team couldn't be accused of entrapment or some other trick to wiggle out of potential charges. If Crazy Harry decided to go along for legal advice while things went down, that could be beneficial as well.

The first time the attorney had offered to go with a group of agents on a sting, it had caught the group supervisor off guard. "I've been at my desk too long. Just put down that I'll be present to give any onsite legal advice as things unroll."

"I don't know, Harry. You'd be an extra body that could be in danger." The supervisor slowly shook his head.

"Oh, come on. You agents get all the action. Let me in on it for once."

The supervisor had finally relented, and Crazy Harry joined the team for a Saturday night bust. The target lived in a sleazy tenement where he sold large quantities of cocaine. An informant had set up a buy for 10:00 p.m. The team was always careful, but tonight they were on extra high alert as the informant had told them the target owned an assault rifle.

Right at 10:00 p.m., the team moved silently toward the apartment door with Crazy Harry somewhere in the midst. The first Special Agent knocked on the door, and when it opened a crack, Crazy Harry snatched a shotgun out of an agent's hands and stormed the apartment yelling, "On the floor right now! Get down, or I'll blow your brains out! You're under arrest!" (It wasn't the scripted response the DEA considered standard, *Mr. X, I'm a federal agent, and I have an arrest warrant*, but effective nonetheless.)

The target instantly dropped to the floor as ordered. He was cuffed, and the team made sure the apartment was secure. Crazy Harry let out a tense sigh and handed the agent back his shotgun. "Hey, thanks a lot. That was really fun," he said as he used the back of his sleeve to mop sweat off his brow.

While it left them with a story to tell, the Special Agents also learned a lesson about bringing someone along like Harry who was not a part of their regular group. It disrupted the flow of the team and can create danger. The whole ordeal was something Fred's team didn't need to be dealing with in the midst of conducting several other cases including that of Katko.

Crazy Harry was constantly prepping for big cases, but he always found time to give teams the legal advice they needed. The gung ho Assistant U.S. Attorney continued to amaze those around him, though he mostly remained locked away in his office writing boring legal paperwork.

CHAPTER
ELEVEN

VINNY KEPT his word and served as the go-between to set up the Katko sting. "Me and my middleman are meeting Katko at a Route 22 roadside diner." Vinny's chest puffed out with pride every time he said *my* middleman or *my* connection, as though this somehow made him the mastermind of the whole setup. "First they'll go over all the final details in the diner. Next they'll drive just down the road to get the marijuana and bring it back to the parking lot, and then the marijuana will be handed off." He tried to give Fred a list of instructions with the diner location, date, time, and where to meet the middleman on the day of the meet. Fred wadded up the paper. Once again, Vinny was trying to insert himself into the operation.

"Vinny, just shut your mouth. You're not an agent. You're a low-life scumbag."

"You're making me feel bad, Fred. You're making me feel bad."

Vinny's morals were as sturdy as shriveled ash. There was no way of knowing who he might have told about the meet. Even if he'd said nothing, any operation involving money and drugs could result in a double-cross with the Special Agents being robbed of their money at gunpoint. There was a certain anxiety caused by knowing that Katko was so good at what he did that his records didn't show so much as a misdemeanor. The troubling sign was that they were meeting him in the middle of the day. Most of the riffraff they dealt with were night creepers who woke up midafternoon and didn't want to meet until dark. The agents were proceeding with full caution for the afternoon setup. They would lack the cover of darkness for the teams to be concealed.

Group 5, Fred's group, worked out of a single large room just like every other group of Special Agents in the DEA. In one corner was the group supervisor's office that had its own door although it was rarely closed. The rest of the area was filled with desks and filing cabinets used by the Special Agents. Toward one side was an open area. Today the open area resembled a war room. The table teemed with men in suits, and a chalkboard stood before Fred who was laying out the sting as though plotting a surprise attack on an enemy battalion. They needed code words and signals (in this case, a cigar), locations needed to be coordinated. He drew rectangles to demonstrate where the cars would be positioned at and near the diner. "One team will move in for the bust while the other team acts as security and watches for trouble or anyone looking suspicious. When the pot arrives, we move in and take 'em."

There were weapons to procure and money for the flash roll. In a huge cement-walled area of the building there was a gun vault. Any agent could take out a shotgun but needed to be certified to get a semi-automatic rifle. Two of the agents signed out these high-velocity rifles for tomorrow's sting. Also behind the gun vault was another secure chamber with millions of dollars in cash. Specific amounts of this money could be signed out to be used for flash rolls. Some of it was from seized money that might eventually make its way to the U.S. Treasury. Fred went down his mental checklist making sure everything was in place.

The New Jersey State Police would be out of sight but nearby in case they ran into big trouble. He went over and over the plan but couldn't shake the bad feeling he got from this middle-of-the-day sting. His mind was fine-tuned for nighttime hijinks. He found himself thinking, *the best-laid plans of mice and men often go awry.*

CHAPTER
TWELVE

NEW YORK/NEW JERSEY
March 15, 1977

THE MORNING of the Katko sting brought clear sunny skies over New York City. At the office, Fred was focusing on the win in the same way he'd seen his coaches prep for one of the numerous high-stakes basketball games he'd played in college. His head was throbbing from lack of sleep. Extra cups of coffee fueled his adrenaline rush, and waves of nerves washed over him and the other Special Agents who, to Fred's surprise, had all arrived by 8:30 a.m. Unusual since they usually didn't get in until 10 or 11, but not because they had a short workday. Quite the opposite. Since most drug deals occurred at night, arriving at noon still required over a 12-hour day. The only benefit was not having to fight daily commuter traffic at 8:00 a.m.

Vinny arrived at 10:00 a.m. with an update: Katko was bringing two "associates" with him. Prior to this, Fred had checked with the DMV to find out what vehicles Katko owned, which turned out to be a blue Cadillac and a black Ford van. They were counting on having a lookout spot one of these vehicles as it rolled to the buy site, but now Katko was suddenly bringing new people into the mix. Would they drive one of their vehicles, and why did he want them along? For his own protection or to help with a rip-off? Fred's first partner had died during a rip-off, and the necessity of being overly cautious would forever stay on the edge of his brain.

The plans had to move forward, so everyone grabbed their gear and started to leave.

Debbie, one of the secretaries, called out as they left, "Make sure you get home tonight." It was her standard heartfelt goodbye.

They went outside, got in several different vehicles, and set off for Jersey. A tan car driven by the UC, Frank Marino, also contained Vinny and the large sum of cash for a flash roll, so one security car followed them. Their plan was to pick up Vinny's friend, a half-assed wise guy who was the middleman Katko trusted, and drive through the Lincoln Tunnel to New Jersey.

While they did this, Fred and another Special Agent picked up a New Jersey state trooper, Kenny, who would stay in the car with them as backup. They parked near the diner. The primary goal of the surveillance units was to protect the undercover agent, plus the informant, and then the money. At least that's what the training manual said. Fred felt differently. "Your number one job is to protect the UC, and the money if you can. Vinny can fend for himself."

The UC was wired with a transmitter, as was his car. Every spoken word would be monitored by Fred and Hatch and the first surveillance car. When the UC got close to the diner, one of the on-site teams would enter and take a seat, posing as customers stopping for a meal. They could observe the meeting; they'd look for signs of trouble and backed up the UC, if needed. Although it all sounded well-planned, these jobs almost never worked without some difficulties. Transmitters failed, surveillance units were in the wrong place, the targets changed delivery arrangements. So Fred was on hyper alert. He sipped more coffee, surprised to notice how intense the smell of coffee beans was in the hot steam.

The Special Agents in the third surveillance car lay in wait like predators at a watering hole. It was their job to look for countersurveillance and be wary of signs that a rip-off was in the works. The last point was especially important because every agent had to remember that these were unknown subjects who had to be considered potentially dangerous. The UC's car contained the cash, so any overheard conversation that indicated a problem would cause the meeting to be aborted immediately. The fact that Katko had requested a daytime meeting added to the irregularity of the sting.

Finally the radio crackled. "501 to all units in the vicinity of the meet. The twenty-five is about ten minutes away. The stool is in the front seat and the middleman in the rear—white male, maybe forty to forty-five years old. Black hair and wearing a light blue sports jacket. Everyone copy?" The radio crackled again with all three units acknowledging the information. Two-five was code for the UC. They had to be very guarded when communicating by radio since anything they said could potentially be intercepted.

The team of agents entered the diner and posed as customers, ready to back up the UC if things went bad.

Within fifteen minutes, Fred spotted Katko's car and reached for his radio. "I think our guys just arrived. They're in a blue Cadillac with Jersey plates—Bravo, Whiskey, Charlie, six, one, seven." Then the three men emerged from the car and headed into the diner. "And," Fred added, "the two guys with him look like pro linebackers."

The crackled conversations coming through the UC's transmitter sounded hopeful at first. The deal was going as expected, until Katko suddenly insisted he would only complete the deal in two separate 500-pound transactions. He had 500 pounds in a van nearby and another 500 a few minutes away. He added that it was his last 1,000 pounds of marijuana.

Fred's heart sank. His disappointment quickly turned to anger. "That little prick," he muttered. Vinny's supposed 50,000 pounds of pot was dwindling before their eyes. There would be no huge bust. Once again, the crooked stool had blown the whole thing out of proportion.

Marino's transmitter cut out briefly, then Fred heard Katko say he wouldn't move the first 500 pounds until it was paid for and one of the linebackers had left with the money. Marino knew that couldn't happen, and it threw a twist into the plans. He tried to hold out for the whole 1,000 pounds. "I thought it would be one load. I only have one van ready to go. I'm a prudent person, you have to understand. I don't want to be in a vehicle like a sitting duck with 500 pounds in my van and $200,000 in cash, waiting to get robbed, while someone goes and gets the other 500 pounds.

But Katko didn't buy his argument and wouldn't budge. Marino had to make the decision to go with Katko's only offer. He reasoned that they would have a shot at getting the other 500 pounds then could possibly use Katko to flip on whoever was above him. Suddenly there was silence. The transmitter had stopped working.

Five minutes passed. Then ten. It was taking too long. Fred's partner lifted his arms above his head to stretch, revealing patches of sweat. Fred took another glance at his watch. Finally, the diner door opened, and Marino emerged with one of the linebackers. Marino led the man to the trunk of his vehicle to check out the money, and the linebacker spent a full ten minutes flipping through every pack of bills. Convinced that Marino was truly a customer, the deal went through. The van filled with 500 pounds of marijuana was brought to the parking lot where Katko then showed the goods to Marino. Marino exited the van, pulled a cheap cigar out of his pocket, and lit it.

That was the signal, he'd seen the product. An adrenaline rush surged through Fred the second that orange ember sparked to life. The agents reacted quickly, moving in like actors on a stage with each knowing their role and placement. Katko was cuffed and in the back of a government car, where the big tough drug dealer sat, hands covering his face, and sobbing like a baby.

It was one of the last times they'd use the cigar signal. It had become too well known, and the Mob especially was leery of anyone with a Havana in their pocket.

Then there was that nagging concern that all of the hard work they'd put in could end up being derailed. Even if they did find the head of the beast, there was no guarantee the person would get prosecuted. Fred and Hatch had met with the Assistant United States Attorney a few weeks ago after completing an intensive investigation and pulling off a superb sting on a drug dealer supplying half of Manhattan, but the prosecutor refused to indict the man. Fred had seen this game before. High level attorneys with big egos and lofty goals for their futures do not want to suffer a defeat in the courtroom. The prosecutor likely saw some slight flaw in the evidence, and refused to risk his career aspirations on a case he might lose.

"You're kidding me!" Fred shook his head in disbelief. "It might not be an easy case, but grow some balls, and do your damn job." He pointed his finger at the prosecutor. "Indict the son-of-a-bitch scumbag."

Hatch had sat back in his chair, relaxed, with his legs crossed and nodded understandingly. The prosecutor refused to indict, and Fred left in an irritated huff while Hatch politely bade him goodbye.

"I'm going to have a heart attack from the stress, and you'll live to be a hundred," Fred said almost accusingly.

"What can you do?" Hatch asked into the air while shrugging his shoulders.

CHAPTER THIRTEEN

FLORIDA
August 7, 1977

G.W. Pridgeon, nineteen years old, and his friend, Lamar English, sixteen years old, had been scuba diving together recreationally for a year. It was the freedom from gravity as well as the thrill of the hunt that drew the two to this favorite spot, a sixty-foot-deep sinkhole large enough to be called a lake. During their lazy descent toward the bottom, they experienced the sensation of floating on air. They'd been here before to search for possible Native American artifacts. The water was murky, and Pridgeon flipped on his diving lantern. A stream of air bubbles rose steadily to the surface while the relaxed sound of the regulators vibrated with each peaceful breath. They skimmed the bottom of the lake, turning over a rock here and there that glowed beneath the small area illuminated by Pridgeon's lantern.

Suddenly, Pridgeon made wild hand motions and English leaned in closer. The two realized that they were looking at vertebrae. Somewhat startled to find this piece of bone, they didn't realize it was human until the beam of the lantern swung upon the decaying skeletal remains that were anchored to cinder blocks next to them. Long hair from a skull swung toward them through the water, and the divers hastily surfaced.

On the fast drive to the sheriff's office in Perry, they talked nervously about their discovery. The skeleton still had flesh and clothing attached, and the dimly lit watery grave had brought to mind the stuff of horror movies. Had they stumbled upon a murder victim?

The sheriff followed them back to the sinkhole, and after much discussion, it was decided that the two divers would go back down with wire cutters. In spite of the shocking discovery, they had made mental notes of exactly where the body was located in the sinkhole. Once they had descended to the skeleton, they realized that each leg was attached to a construction cinder block with electrical wire, and the torso was attached to three blocks. With some work, they managed to free the skeleton and bring it to the surface.

The Leon Sheriff Diving Team was quickly rounded up, and a second skeleton was found fifteen feet farther down the lake. A third skeleton was found in a pond right next to the sinkhole, having been washed along through an underground tunnel that connected the two.

"It was real weird," said one of the boys. "When we were bringing him up, it was as if he was smiling at us. It was almost like he was glad we had found him."

Police were readying to pump the bottom of the sinkhole. They called in a Navy diving team to see what equipment would be needed, and it was during this investigative dive that the fourth set of remains was located.

After that, authorities used dental records, medical histories, and the remaining pieces of clothing to quickly determine that these were the four people who'd gone missing some eight months prior—Harold Sims, Douglas Hood, and Sheila and Sandy McAdams. All were wearing coats or clothing that fit with the weather when they had gone missing eight months earlier. Three had been shot in the head, execution style, but who did this and why? Interviews with the families of the four victims turned up nothing that might help solve the case.

CHAPTER
FOURTEEN

NEW YORK
Mid-1970s

IT WAS ABOUT THIS TIME, when Fred was juggling too many cases at work, that the bosses sent a new transfer his way. Typically when the New York DEA needed more agents, they got them in batches. If they needed ten people, they transferred twenty from other cities knowing that half would quit, especially if they weren't originally from New York. For some it was the sticker shock of finding out that a salary that allowed them the ability to buy a sprawling three-bedroom house in some Indiana suburb would now only stretch far enough for an efficiency apartment in a questionable neighborhood in the Bronx. On top of that, an agent from another division would be joining Group 5. The New York DEA office had nine groups of agents. Each was supposed to consist of fifteen staff members, but due to never being able to get enough people hired, generally there were only twelve Special Agents plus the group supervisor, known as the GS.

The new transfer was originally from Kansas City, so when Fred had to call a friend in that office on a case, he decided to find out more about the new guy. He'd had trouble reaching the friend because everyone in that department was out golfing by 4:00 nearly every afternoon. Not so in the New York office. The endless New York hours were only one reason recruits transferred out after only a few weeks of working in The Big Apple. But today someone in the Kansas office finally answered the phone.

"Tell me about this George Redden. He's been in our New York office awhile now, and he'll be joining my group. So just wondering why he transferred here in the first place?"

There was a short pause. "George is not a bad guy. He just got on the wrong side of the bosses."

Notions flashed through Fred's mind, wondering what this agent may have done. Some mistakes could mean the difference between life and death in this job. "I'd better sit down while you lay out the situation." He hoped his tone implied that the New York agents were too busy to babysit someone who had interfered with the Kansas City agents' cushy hours.

"Well, in hindsight we could probably chalk it up to an agent not realizing it wasn't wise to report a superior for questionable ethical actions. He just could have handled the situation differently."

"So he was correct in what he reported though?"

"Yes, but his interests differed from those of the Special Agent in Charge. Apparently, Redden requested the use of a DEA airplane to help with one of his open cases. He was turned down. Then he found out it was because the Special Agent in Charge used that plane to go to the Colorado Mountains with his girlfriend. Redden should have handled it differently because in cases like this, the main man always wins. He's actually a swell guy, really well-liked around here. So they gave him a second chance. That is why you have him now in New York."

Fred pondered the explanation. Having an error in judgment while on a case was one thing, but what Redden did was understandable. Reporting an incident that interfered with a case was something Fred could accept. He would have to get to know more about this Special Agent Redden.

CHAPTER FIFTEEN

NEW JERSEY/NEW YORK
November 1977

FRED WAS ENJOYING a hearty helping of turkey, stuffing, and potatoes smothered in gravy. He would surely be a three-plater before the meal was complete with pumpkin pie. Twenty-five guests flowed through the house, including Special Agent Redden. Fred hadn't been able to stomach the thought of his new friend eating chicken chow mein in a basement apartment or the front seat of his car. He'd explained the story to Ginger who insisted Redden join them. When Fred extended the invitation, Redden responded with the enthusiasm of a teenage girl at the mall with her dad's credit card. He'd readily accepted and offered to bring wine, beer, food, or anything else. Fred assured him Ginger had everything under control and to just show up.

Redden came two hours early with roses, two bottles of wine, and a basketball. Fred didn't ask about the basketball but happily tossed it in the corner. Fred quickly discovered that Redden was not only cordial, but had an engaging sense of humor. By the time the meal was served, Redden was several drinks into a bottle of hard liquor, but the redeeming part was the fact that he was a happy drunk.

Ginger was extra joyful today. Fred had taken tomorrow off so the two of them could spend the day together and start their Christmas shopping. Currently Ginger was sitting at the table showing off baby Dave, now seven months old, to the relatives, and regaling their company with a story about the baby's antics the other day, when ringing from the next room caused Fred to pause mid-bite. Wondering who would be interrupting their family Thanksgiving, he moseyed over to the phone.

"Hey, Fred, sorry to bother you, but I got some good news, and I'll make it quick." It was Kenny, one of the New Jersey state troopers. "I got a call from the lawyer, and our man Katko had a change of heart. He's decided to cooperate rather than go to Trenton State Prison for a whole lot of years."

Fred shut the door, drowning out the raucous laughter from the other room. "As I remember it, you offered him a chance after we arrested him, and he told you to screw yourself. Wouldn't even give up the other 500 pounds we'd expected to find. He wanted to play hard ball."

"You got it, Fred, but now Katko says he's scared of the 'big guys.' Says he thinks they'll kill him and his family."

"What does the scumbag have to offer?" Fred questioned, thinking of the mouth-watering meal turning cold at the table.

"You'll have to talk to him."

"We better check him out. Can I meet with Katko?"

"Yeah, his lawyers want to meet tomorrow. At his office. In Colonia. 9:00 a.m."

Fred groaned. "Ginger won't be happy. I'm supposed to take the day off, but I'll meet you at nine."

Kenny continued. "If you can, bring that Wimpy the Worm guy. What's his name, Vinny?"

"Vinny, The Cat? Can't do," Fred said clicking a pen nub against the paper on which he was writing notes. "You didn't hear what happened?"

"Nope, tell me."

"Vinny is no longer with us in body; he's in spirit only and probably a possessed one at that. Used up all of his nine lives."

"You're kidding! If someone had told me, I'd have gone to his funeral…and pissed on his head."

Fred wasn't surprised to hear it. Vinny had made more enemies than friends during his life. "Yeah, The Cat stopped at a bar in Queens. He had a few drinks, got up, and left. According to a few witnesses, some guy just walked up and put three round holes in his head. While Vinny's pouring blood all over the sidewalk, the guy reaches down and swipes his money—or should I say the government's money."

"Did they catch the guy?"

"Nope. NYPD figured it was a robbery gone bad and wrote it up as such. That's what I heard anyway. Who knows? Maybe he just up and died, and it's just another lie."

"They should have classified it as rodent extermination."

"But hey, The Cat did help you get a Cadillac due to government confiscation."

"You know something, Fred. That damn car broke down every week until I dumped it. It was as dysfunctional as The Cat."

"Yep, figures." Fred finished talking then happily returned to his Thanksgiving meal.

———

IT WASN'T until company had cleared out, the dishes were done, and the kids were in bed that he worked up the courage to tell Ginger he'd be gone for a few hours the next day. Redden was passed out on the couch, which meant Fred would know where to find him for their meeting with Katko tomorrow. It also caused him to reflect on the old adage Special Agents often repeated: DEA is a hundred alcoholics trying to catch a thousand drug addicts.

Hatch would be dealing with another of the many open cases tomorrow, or he would have been Fred's partner. Though skilled at interviewing, Fred wondered how much of an asset the hungover Redden would be the next day.

"I'll be home by noon," he told Ginger.

She was not happy.

"I promise. Noon."

It wasn't that she didn't believe *his* promises. It was always someone else who disrupted the plans. Fred had once been sent down to a southern state for three days. "I may not be able to contact you much when I'm gone," he'd explained, knowing it wouldn't do much to ease her concern. But then the Special Agents were unexpectedly diverted to South America. Due to the extremely dangerous nature of the operation and the subjects of the investigation, Fred was not able to call Ginger. Fred was in a jungle working sixteen-hour days with nothing but a few huts and no telephones. Three days turned into four days, and then a week. Through relentless persistence, Ginger was able to find out that Fred had been sent to a country dominated by drug cartels.

She had been forced to suddenly face the harsh realities of life as a DEA agent's wife. With each passing hour, she became more certain that her husband would not be returning. Had he been tortured to death? Caught off guard and shot before even having time to contemplate the child (they had Suzie at the time) he'd be leaving behind? How would she tell her young daughter? On the ninth day, she contacted his group supervisor. What were the steps one followed when one's husband didn't return from a mission? The nights were sleepless. The happy face she had continued presenting to Suzie each morning didn't match the helplessness and distress that churned inside. On the twelfth day, she got word that Fred was on his way back. She sank into a chair and wept uncontrollably, finally allowing herself to release the pent-up emotions.

Ginger realized it was hard on her husband as well. He wasn't one to dwell on his emotions, but she knew he occasionally harbored some regrets about leaving teaching. Being an agent meant sacrifice and loneliness. As much as she worried about and missed him, he missed his family when he was gone for days and weeks at a time. During the times he was on a mission where he couldn't contact Ginger, it seemed to border on cruelty. Yet, she admired the way he managed to remain so upbeat in spite of the job demands and pressure.

He promised her once more before they fell asleep. "Noon."

⊏⊐

FRED TRIED to get right to the point with Katko and his lawyers, but they had other ideas. It took Fred and Redden forty-five minutes just to explain to people who should have known better that the government would not recommend a sentence. The best he could do was notify the sentencing judge that Katko had cooperated.

Katko was almost childlike when he started telling his story. Every sentence began with some long-winded excuse about why he didn't really want to become a drug dealer in the first place and how his involvement was minimal. And he had been *so* desperate, anyone in his shoes would have done the same thing.

"Look Charles, this is getting us nowhere. You have already pled guilty to conspiracy to import and distribute marijuana. I don't give a damn why you did it or how sorry you are. So let's cut through the bullshit." Fred's anxiety was increasing with each movement of the clock inching closer to noon.

Katko hung his head. "I guess I'll start at the beginning."

He did, and went all the way to the end, giving names (twenty in all), locations, and dates. He told about a farm in Georgia, and drugs shipped to Tennessee. A man named Raymond Hawkins and his wife Karen. Hawkins had told him about a man who went by the name Muscles and some other guy with a lot of money who financed the operation. There were drug-laden shrimp boats coming in on southern beaches. He gave details on every load he'd picked up and delivered. Where the horse farms were located, and which banks were used. It involved big businessmen out of Texas with their own tractor trailers, private planes, and boats. Even their own warehouses. If his story turned out to be true, it would be one of the largest smuggling operations in U.S. history, and certainly the most sophisticated. If that happened, it didn't break Fred's heart that Vinny wouldn't be around to collect his promised reward. Fred had the names Katko gave him entered into NADDIS. One unusual name stood curiously apart from the others: Charles "Muscles" Foster.

There would have been no way for Fred to predict the series of events that would follow from the act of simply entering the names into NADDIS as he'd done many times before.

By 1:00 p.m. they were finished. Fred would use the twenty-five-minute drive home to devise the best way to appease Ginger. Extra hugs, extra snuggles watching TV, and maybe an unexpected gift for her when they went Christmas shopping.

CHAPTER
SIXTEEN

NEW YORK
Early 1970s

WHEN A WEEKEND WASN'T FILLED with surveillance or other urgent business, the Group 5 Special Agents and their wives got together on Long Island for cookouts—or cook-ins during those dreaded winter months. They not only worked together but socialized together (like family but without that degree of dysfunction). The men understood the stress and demands of each other's jobs. The potential for alcohol abuse was high among these agents who experienced excessive anxiety, worked long hours, had impaired sleep, and lived daily with the threat of death. However, most of the wives were shielded from getting a clear picture of the risks and pressure their husbands faced.

During summer months, they'd hook up an oversized yellow inflatable raft to the back of a boat and bring it to the middle of the Long Island Sound. While the children remained in the care of the teenage kids, the adults would load up in the raft and anchor it in the water. Then they'd take turns water skiing or tubing while one person drove the boat—usually one of the women since the men were busy passing around the plastic gallon jug of Harvey Wallbangers. Since it was a big shore house with many bedrooms, all the families would spend the night.

Fred scrutinized Ginger from across the room in the spacious ranch-style house of one of his coworkers. How had he ever gotten so lucky? He walked outside to tend to the "men's job" of turning the hamburgers and hot dogs—for Fred, of course, it was hot dogs—on the grill while the women prepared macaroni salads and refereed the antics of the eight energetic children. The men discussed in hushed tones their disappointment and anger at being denied their request last month at a budget meeting—bulletproof vests, which would have been easily obtainable. Most of them had thought these high-priority items for protection would be approved with ease, especially in comparison to multimillions spent on other aspects of the operations.

Fred remained optimistic. They would put in the request again for bulletproof vests next quarter. For now, he wanted to focus on a rare relaxing weekend with his family and friends. It brought him joy to hear Ginger's voice rise above the laughter circling from the kitchen.

"Yep! Next week our guys will be out there again playing big boy cops and robbers and putting on their Hopalong Cassidy outfits!" the women tittered, stacking plates and mixing pitchers of Kool-Aid.

"I don't know who likes playing dress-up more—my son or my husband! He straps on his gun and holster with the same enthusiasm that my kids do with their western set," one of the wives said with good-natured teasing.

The men didn't mind the light-hearted jabs, and occasionally joined in by reminding the ladies that they'd caught a "big-boy smuggler" last week.

At first, it was exciting for the wives to have Special Agent husbands with their mysterious well-respected government positions. Ginger had even used this to finagle their way into the White House following Fred's graduation from the training academy.

"Hey, let's go see where the president lives," Ginger had announced after they'd spent a morning looking at the Washington, D.C., museums."

"You can't just go to the White House," Fred had explained. "You have to set it up ahead of time. They do background checks."

But Ginger had insisted and then proceeded to the entrance with Fred in tow explaining to the lady working there that her husband was a government Special Agent. The woman had called over an official-looking guard who'd examined Fred's DEA credentials, and within minutes the couple had joined a group just starting their tour.

It took time for the wives to realize that behind the glamour awaited real threats. But today was not a day to dwell on the dangers of the job. The women were too busy doting on Bonnie and gushing over her engagement ring. In one month she would be Mrs. Russell Moretti, the proud wife of one of Fred's former partners. It would be a much-needed joyous event for all of them to attend the wedding and fully welcome Bonnie into their fold. But that levity was not to be long-lived.

The next month, Russell was on a drug sting with an informant at a sleazy hotel when the situation went bad. Assisting Russell was thirty-two-year-old Special Agent Tommy Devine who was in the next room secretly monitoring the situation, and there was an adjoining door in case Russell needed backup. Russell was to meet with the targets to purchase a large amount of drugs, and then make the arrest. The two targets, Jose Nieves and Jose Mata, talked with Russell and confirmed there was cash for the buy. The drug dealers left the motel room for a short time but returned later with the intention of robbing Russell of the $160,000. There was some commotion that made Tommy decide to burst through the connecting door. He got into a scuffle with one of the targets, and a gun went off hitting Tommy in the leg and causing him to crumple to the floor. One of the assailants stood over Tommy and put one cold-blooded bullet through his neck, paralyzing him from the chest down. At about the same time, Russell jumped onto the motel bed, pulled out his own pistol, and a raging gun battle ensued among Russell and the two Joses. Russell hit and wounded one of the assailants, but not before one of their bullets struck Russell in the chest, killing him instantly. As the two Joses tried to flee, Special Agents who were stationed throughout the hotel confronted them, and another fiery gunfight took place. No Special Agents were injured in that shootout, but the two Joses were shot dead. The full details were never released to Bonnie or the other Special Agents.

When Ginger heard the devastating news, she had come face to face with the world she and the other wives lived in. Any of them might be the next Bonnie.

"I can't stand it," she'd confided to Fred at the funeral. "All I can think about is Bonnie and how her beautiful wedding dress will still be hanging in the closet on the day the two of them would have become one." It had gone unspoken between them that it could just as easily have been Fred in that casket.

A FEW WEEKS later there was an all-agents meeting in the New York office. The Special Agent in Charge spoke, as did a DEA attorney who had been brought in from headquarters to address the recent shooting and the repercussions of not having bulletproof vests. Not only had Fred's first partner died, but a 32- year-old agent was paralyzed from mid-chest down, and the informant and his two scumbag friends were dead. As a group, the New York agents were outraged. They'd been asking for vests for years, to no avail. The meeting became heated with Special Agents shouting out their opposition to what the attorney had to say.

"You piss away money on picnics but not to protect a twenty-five year-old guy—who's dead now!" someone shouted. Most meetings were civil, but this one had the agents' blood boiling.

Tommy O'Grady was a former attorney turned Special Agent. Everyone referred to him as O.G., which for some reason seemed to fit the tall strapping Irishman. He had put much time into the request for the agents to receive protective vests. He'd used his legal knowledge to help plead his case, and he had not given up on finding a way to get this vital protection. "Russell could be alive today if that request had been approved!"

The bowtie-wearing attorney from headquarters smirked with self-satisfaction while taking off his jacket to reveal red suspenders. He sat down and rolled up the shirtsleeves of a garishly striped shirt, then paused and ran a hand atop his oiled comb-over and said with a thin smile, "Well, men, you're supposed to be so tough. My recommendation would be to put on a couple extra t-shirts when you're out there!"

It was too soon for a joke in such poor taste, especially one that came down hard on the heels of their comrade's death.

O.G. flew to his feet and took angry strides toward the attorney. "I'm gonna rip your suspenders off, stick 'em up your ass...and pull 'em out your throat!" he bellowed as several agents stepped in to hold him back.

The attorney stood rigidly. "Hey, I was just trying to make a funny," he said, trying to brush it off with a nervous chuckle.

One year later they got the vests. And soon after, a memo. The supervisor directed them not to wear the vests due to their poor quality—they would only stop a .22 and maybe a .25 bullet. Certainly, the agents were told, they were useless against a 9mm or a .32 It was another slap in the face for the Special Agents.

CHAPTER
SEVENTEEN

TEXAS
Early 1960s

BENEATH BRIGHT LIGHTS, the crowded stands buzzed with excited talk. Texans in their finest western wear waited impatiently while the clock ticked as the much-talked-about horse, Cutter Bill, strained beneath its rider who was waiting to enter the arena. The crowd of horse-loving Texans cheered enthusiastically as Cutter Bill and rider galloped toward a group of alert cattle, dust kicking up behind the agile horse who quickly began maneuvering a determined steer back toward the holding pen. Tension built as the seconds ticked down. The crowd was in awe.

Cutter Bill was being judged on his ability to swiftly move a steer to a place of the rider's choosing. It's a skill left over from the old cattle drive days when cows needed to be separated from the herd. This particular quarter horse with a telling white star on his forehead wowed the spectators with his skill and relentless determination. No doubt that many of those in the stands found themselves wishing they could claim Cutter Bill as their own. One of those people was Charles Foster, a scrawny ranch hand who fancied the good life. With oversized ears that mushroomed from a smallish head, and a squeaky too-excited voice, Charles's friends had taken to calling him "Muscles" as an ironic nickname. He weighed no more than 130 pounds and was not much over five feet tall, but seemed shorter since he walked bent over. It was the way his body was molded from riding too many bucking broncos and bulls. Muscles turned to the older gentleman next to him and yelled with enthusiasm, "That's one hell of a great cutting horse! The best I've seen."

"He sure is," the man replied proudly. The horse had been winning nearly every competition he'd been in. The man was Rex Cauble, owner of Cutter Bill, and role model to Muscles who idolized this suave Texan whose name meant something to people in these parts. Rex, blessed with a strong jaw and savvy eyes, exuded confidence. He gave Muscles a fatherly pat on the back. Few would have ever figured the two would end up in what some considered a puzzling relationship. When the two had first been introduced in 1960—an ominous meeting if ever there was one—something about Muscles had immediately piqued the older man's curiosity. Both men, while vastly different in appearance, demeanor, and achievements, had a deep love for horses.

One of the first questions Rex had ever asked Muscles was, "Do you know much about quarter horses?" Rex did not and he knew it. He had an expansive fortune and some impressive quarter horses but lacked the knowledge he needed to become the legendary horseman he dreamed of becoming.

Muscles had let out a low whistle. "Horses have been my life. I've been a ranch hand and bronco rider since I was a kid." His voice was timid and squeaky, which many found annoying, but this barely registered with Rex, who only seemed able to focus on Muscles's genuine enthusiasm; this character trait resonated with Rex. Muscles had grown up surrounded by the rodeo world and was a gifted wheeler and dealer as well. Muscles had a fire burning inside of him to be great at something. From a lifetime of rodeo and ranch work, he'd turned into one of the best horse trainers in Texas.

By the end of the day, Rex had offered his new mentee a job

breaking and breeding horses on one of his ranches. Muscles had gladly accepted, not fully realizing his good fortune in being brought into the realm of Rex Cauble's immense empire. Almost immediately, there had been an undeniable chemistry between the two; each so different from the other that at a glance no one would have expected a friendship to form, much less the type of intense bond that would eventually define their relationship. It could have been a case study delving into raw natural human tendencies. At its core was the competitive nature of two people from humble beginnings and their quest to compete for the limited resources of money, power, and women.

Born in Vaughan, Texas, in 1913 to cotton-farmer parents who taught him the value of hard work, Rex was never expected to leave his humble beginnings. As a young man he kept his eyes open for opportunity, and when opportunity met hard work, Rex clawed his way to the top, never shying away from a risk if there was a healthy chance for a windfall at the end. (Risk would be both his path out of poverty as well as his eventual downfall.) He got his start as a rough-neck at seventeen, then a driller, and finally a tool pusher (a term used in the oil business for someone who manages a team of workers) before buying a drill rig on credit and becoming a wildcatter, drilling for oil in spots not known to be oil fields.

His biggest financial windfall came from marrying Josephine Sterling, a wealthy widow. When Rex greatly exaggerated his own wealth to Josephine, she believed him and thought they'd be combining their fortunes into a financial empire. Rex was always one step ahead. He adopted the son who Josephine had previously adopted herself and named him Lewis Rex Cauble. Then he took control over Josephine's riches. All of their businesses were sheltered under the name Cauble Enterprises. Eventually, he did become a self-made millionaire by expanding his efforts into the oil and gas business, a welding supply company, bank holdings—another double-edged sword—and eventually eleven ranches. Then came his pride and joy, the Cutter Bill's Western World stores.

He walked among the Texas elite—wealthy businessmen, executives, and well-known politicians. Rex understood the importance of rubbing shoulders with the upper crust. It set him above others. One of his 1,400-acre ranches was jointly owned with his close friend, State District Judge Byron Matthews. He even had associations with Governor John Connally, who had been seriously wounded while riding in the limousine with President Kennedy the day he was assassinated. He counted Bob Hope and cowboy actors Roy Rogers and John Wayne among his close friends.

Rex held a high regard for law enforcement and became a member of the Special Texas Rangers. He was a fervent anti-marijuana crusader who made and paid for his own anti-drug radio commercials. In the mid-1970s, his son, Lewis, was treated at the Center for Behavioral Studies at North Texas State University for what Rex considered to be an addiction to marijuana. Soon after, Rex paid for Willie Nelson, of all people, to come and play a benefit concert to raise funds for the center. He required prospective employees to pass lie-detector tests to determine if they'd ever taken drugs. If they had, he wouldn't hire them. State law officials knew they could come to Rex if they needed someone to cover a flash roll of money for an undercover drug sting. He even loaned them his personal jet and pilot. Of course, it didn't hurt to have close ties with these agencies in his endless quest to secure important connections, and to ease his paranoia about people taking advantage of him.

But Rex's true passion in life was horses, and what a horse Cutter Bill was to be passionate about; no doubt he was a "one-in-a-million horse," evidenced by him going on to win numerous rodeo events before hitting the big time when he won the National Cutting Horse Association world title. Though Rex at first didn't have the experience or skill of others when it came to horses, he was an ardent fan of the cowboy life. It was in honor of his horse's world title that Rex had originally opened the Cutter Bill's Western World stores, which carried a prestigious line of Cutter Bill's western clothing and boots. Celebrities frequented the store, and it wasn't uncommon to find four-digit price tags among the designer clothing. They offered a limited-edition golden ermine fur cowboy hat for $2,500, alligator boots for $2,500, and a four-inch solid gold stickpin of a cowboy holding a diamond gun for

$3,500. As a special touch, there was a bowl of shiny gold matchbooks with the Cutter Bill logo on the front. With the magnificent horse's renowned fame, Cutter Bill became quite popular with the lady horses and went on to father 637 registered foals. Rex's income soared again from the stud fees.

CHAPTER EIGHTEEN

TEXAS
1976

PERHAPS BEING a con man and a shrewd bargainer went together in a ribs-and-barbeque kind of way. Muscles's ability to make people believe whatever story he decided upon was a definite bonus in upselling a horse he was unloading, or downplaying one he wanted to buy. The first time he travelled to a southern ranch to conduct some quarter horse business, he made sure he rubbed shoulders with the ranch owner, Raymond Hawkins. Though they'd initially met four years ago, Hawkins had since been in prison on drug-related charges. This time Hawkins enticed Muscles to come to Georgia under the pretense of needing someone to break horses. Muscles had a special knack for endearing himself to the wealthy who seemed to all have the same insatiable need for praise, like a spoiled child. Through this new friendship, Muscles soon realized that Hawkins, though still considered a young man, had lots of cash as well as material luxuries. The good life was an immediate lure for Muscles who yearned to mingle with the upper crust. He was well liked but never in the spotlight that he desired. He made friends easily enough but had a nagging feeling it was partly due to his small stature; other men found him nonthreatening.

Muscles had not cornered the market on cunningness, however. Shrewdness was also Hawkins's shadow. He quickly surmised that Muscles had the characteristics of someone he could gently pull into the addicting world of drug trafficking. When he found out that Muscles had access to horse barns, horse trailers, and virtually empty ranches, his pockets started buzzing with the thought of lining them with even more cash that could be made through the use of this unsightly little cowpoke. Muscles *thought* he could out-con anyone, and Hawkins was ready to use that belief to his benefit. He'd make sure Muscles thought he was getting the better end of the bargain, though it would not be true. He promised Muscles $20,000 to help with the drug-smuggling venture, an offer Muscles readily accepted before the offer was fully out of Hawkins's mouth. Thus, Raymond Hawkins made a new connection for the drug-distribution business.

CHAPTER
NINETEEN

TENNESSEE/FLORIDA
August 1976–1977

SO IT WAS in August of 1976 that Muscles dipped his toes into the waters of drug smuggling. He told Poppa Rex Cauble that he was going into the shrimping business with his friends in Georgia and convinced The Old Man to lend him money to buy a shrimp boat, the *Monkey*, from Port Aransas boat broker, Russel Galjour. From Rex, Muscles got enough for the $10,000 down payment, which he gave to Carlos Gerdes, the suave business mogul, in hundred-dollar bills. Gerdes's friend, reclusive millionaire John Ruppel, paid the remainder of the $148,000 cost, with the condition he receive a cut of the profits, but he had some hesitations. Which of them had experience shrimping? Though eccentric with his shoulder-length gray-white hair and hippie-like demeanor, sixty-one-year-old Ruppel had a keen eye for overseeing details of his businesses from the mountaintop mansion he owned known as "The Castle."

"We have people experienced in bringing in these 'loads,'" Gerdes and Muscles assured him.

It didn't take Muscles long to copywrite the lines he'd use to lure others into helping where he needed them. "There's big money in the smuggling business. And no risk on your part. You let me take that on." This mantra became his standard come-on to convince others to join in for a share of the profits. He had a feel for the type of personality that could be hooked with thoughts of easy money.

It was with these same words that Muscles convinced his friend Willis Judge Butler to carry out a small yet significant job. Butler needed to scour the coast to find places where the boats could land. Places that could accommodate a large trawler yet were secluded, but not so secluded that they were too far from warehouses and barns where the marijuana would be stored. He found places in Florida, Texas, Georgia, and Louisiana. Muscles had promised him big money for his services and for helping to unload the boats once they arrived.

When they later acquired the shrimper *Agnes Pauline*, Butler moved up the illegal corporate ladder and was given the job of outfitting the shrimper to the tune of $46,000. It was not a simple job and would ultimately be met with disagreement that nearly led to a murder.

RUPPEL HAD to have an inkling that the boat was bringing in too much money, but Gerdes suspected he was blinded by dollar signs. Then Muscles and Gerdes had an idea. Gerdes turned to friend Martin Sneed, Sr., and said, "We need receipts showing that the *Monkey* sold shrimp or fish. You can get that done." Sneed, a shipbuilder who was familiar with all things sea-related took the $3,500 Gerdes gave him for the assignment.

It didn't take long for Sneed to get a phony receipt of sale, and then they were all satisfied that Ruppel would continue to fund their "shrimp boat" business, once he could convince himself the *Monkey* was being used to bring in shrimp rather than marijuana.

THE FIRST BOATLOAD on the *Monkey* came February 1977 and the second the end of May. They had sent the shrimper to Colombia with millions of dollars stored inside scuba tanks. Hawkins, Muscles,

Gerdes, and Charles Talkington, one of Rex's ranch hands, were there to unload it. From the southeast port in Texas, they took the bales of marijuana to ranches near Meridian, Crockett, and Denton—all owned by Rex Cauble. Muscles paid the ranch foreman to take a two-week vacation but didn't tell him it was so the smugglers could use the barns to store marijuana while they distributed the drugs from the *Monkey*. It was Butler and Talkington who drove two truckloads all the way to Newport, Tennessee.

And who was there to direct them every step of the way? Muscles. He'd quickly risen up the ranks by demonstrating the ability to orchestrate the operation. He had trucks and men ready to unload the shipment and knew where each refrigerated truck (rented under a phony name) would head with the marijuana. Hawkins was finding it increasingly challenging to smuggle drugs in Georgia and Florida due to new drug laws. In fact, by the spring of 1977, they'd started moving the operation from Georgia to Texas. Hawkins was so taken in by the cowboy atmosphere that he even started wearing a ten-gallon hat. When Muscles suggested he move to Texas, Hawkins did, and bought the half-million-dollar Cherokee Ranch from Rex. He made a $100,000 down payment in cash, which Rex agreed not to claim on his tax return. Hawkins was up to his eyeballs in cash and bought the *Bayou Blues* shrimp boat. He also made trips to Las Vegas for gambling sprees and to launder money as "winnings." Benny Binion, the famous Las Vegas casino owner, was a close friend of Rex's. It was suspected that Rex used this friendship to allow him easy access to launder money as gambling winnings.

Muscles's services were so vital that Hawkins paid him $250,000, part of which was to be used for costs such as transporting the loads. Hawkins was taken aback when Muscles eagerly split the money in half right in front of him and presented it to Rex Cauble, in the way a dog would drop a bone in its master's lap. Rex looked pleased. He put the money in an envelope, which he labeled with the name of one of his companies, McVane Steel. Since late 1976, Cauble Enterprises had been sinking further into debt. Business conditions and the economy took a bad turn in the early 1970s. The oil crises of 1973–1974 hit Rex hard. Many of his businesses took a dive.

Rex wasn't questioning where the money came from. Both men had a weak spot: Rex an insatiable desire for power and control and Muscles an obsession with women.

Though Muscles had been unable to acquire his own riches, through Rex he became rich by association. It was no casual association. Rex quickly became a father figure to Muscles. It was a narrow wire on which Muscles walked. There was a vein of bad temper that ran straight through Rex, top to bottom. Rex gave an ass-chewing like no other, and some of his hired hands quit on account of it. But Muscles responded with humility. On one hand, Poppa Rex would give him money for anything he wanted. Yet on the other hand, the multimillionaire insisted on seeing and approving every bill that was paid. There was something unspoken between the two. Rex had to have willful ignorance toward Muscles's "business" affairs, yet he was also blinded by his own need for Muscles's obedience and adoration. It was because of this that Muscles frequently threatened those beneath him with what would happen if Rex got wind of the operation.

CHAPTER
TWENTY

TEXAS
Mid-1970s

THE SOMEWHAT STARTLED aviation salesman ushered an unexpected customer into the covered showroom, which was more a makeshift hangar than anything. Better than most, he understood that buying a private plane was the ultimate symbol of wealth and prestige for a businessman in the 1970s. It was not a simple process though. His exclusive well-dressed customers would start by researching various airplane models and manufacturers, considering factors such as performance, range, and cabin size. As a general rule, they tended to present themselves as experts in the field whose knowledge was equivalent to his, an aviation expert. Many times he had to challenge claims of the same airplane being available in some nearby state for thousands of dollars less; these were shrewd customers. He shrugged it off, chalking it up to their fiercely competitive drive that got them to the position that enabled them to even purchase a personal aircraft.

So, it was beneath this backdrop that he was caught off guard by a gentleman wearing a pair of cutoffs and a t-shirt who had arrived unexpectedly (most had private secretaries who booked an appointment to ensure that Mr. Bigshot wouldn't be kept waiting for even a moment). With a firm handshake, the man introduced himself.

"Raymond Hawkins. Cherokee Ranch," the man said as though out of all the thousands of Texas ranches, the salesman would no doubt be jubilantly familiar with this one.

They made small talk. The salesman focused the conversation on Hawkins. He had doubts as to the man's authenticity based on so many irregularities, not the least being the hippie-type sandals he was wearing. Still, fact could be stranger than fiction, and he didn't want to miss out on a potential sale. *These types thrive on being the center of attention*, he had well learned. "Are you a pilot?"

"No, sir. I have a man who works for me who'll be doing the flying. Got business in Tennessee, and upstate New York." He then opened the door, climbing into a Beechcraft and looking around but didn't ask questions, so the salesman shared important details—top speed, operating cost per hour, and so on. The man nodded imperceptibly and moved on to another plane and then another.

"We have top-of-the-line customization options in many of our airplanes," the salesman said, assuming that like most customers, Mr. Hawkins would require a specialized interior design, perhaps a bar, or a logo for the exterior. He continued spewing out facts, figures, and opinions hoping to find some topic that would finally lead to that barrage of questions every customer had before settling—sometimes weeks later—on that perfect airplane.

"I'll take this one," Hawkins announced suddenly, pointing to the red-and-white Cessna Skyhawk he'd spent minimal time examining.

"That's a fine machine, sir," the salesman said, removing his sunglasses and pocketing them. He was completely taken aback. "Shall I...er, OK, what bank will you be getting the loan from?"

"I'm not. This is a cash deal. In fact, I'll have someone here with the green in an hour."

The flustered salesman led Hawkins to an office so he could make a phone call, and within the hour a car arrived. The person within handed Hawkins an oversized briefcase filled with hundred-dollar bills. The salesman let out a low whistle then counted the bills into piles on his desk, bewildered the entire time that in all his years as a salesman he had never even heard of an airplane being paid for in cash, especially by someone dressed so casually.

Perhaps something inside him questioned the legitimacy of this much cash, but a sale was a sale, and it wasn't unheard of for people in these parts to have pockets full of oil money. He knew the type well. Money, dinero, green. It was the fuel that drove all the powerful men.

For Hawkins, the prestige of being some top dog who could walk in with a briefcase full of money became addicting. The thrill of the high-roller lifestyle was his drug. Fast horses. Fast women. The fast life. He wanted it all. Although he was married, Hawkins was a womanizer with a girlfriend (who not surprisingly had expensive taste). One day to appease her after an argument, she decided she just had to have a new Mercedes. Hawkins agreed to it hoping he'd avoid another blowup fight. The man at the dealership showed her five cars, each a different color.

She stood for a while in the classic arms-crossed, head-tipped manner of those contemplating something important. But she could not decide. "I'll take them all!" she finally announced with the confidence that comes from being able to snap one's manicured fingers to get what one wants. Hawkins hesitated slightly; it was the price he had to pay for the privilege of being seen about with a beautiful, younger woman. So he paid for the cars. In cash.

In fact, Hawkins had so much drug money lying around that he couldn't keep it all in his home. The possibility of an associate robbing him constantly hung over his head. Plus, he was slightly paranoid, so he took to hiding the money. He tended to consider himself more important than others and started fancying himself a modern-day pirate.

In his hand was a carefully drawn map marked with several big red "Xs" that indicated where he'd buried boxes of money on his property. He tossed the map on the table. His associate Ronnie Ray was here on "business," and he helped Hawkins load bundles of hundreds into four plastic Tupperware containers; the larger boxes could hold upwards of $300,000. When they were full, he applied caulk around the edges and pressed the lids on. That would keep out any moisture. Then after Ronnie Ray unloaded the marijuana he had delivered and left for home, Hawkins went into the brush-covered hillsides to bury his treasure boxes.

One day, a big load of drugs was on its way, and Hawkins needed cash. He took his map and dug up three boxes but couldn't find the location of the fourth box as indicated by the last red X. So when Ronnie Ray arrived with a new load of drugs, the two spent hours digging up the land trying to find the missing box until Hawkins finally threw his shovel down in disgust and announced, "Damn it, I screwed up the map, so to hell with it. I can't waste any more time looking for one box. Someday some kids will be running around out here and find a box with $200,000."

CHAPTER
TWENTY-ONE

FLORIDA
Fall 1977

IT BEGAN one evening with the rain pounding down in sheets, which made the humidity thick as honey. This type of weather always brought Ronnie Ray bad fortune. It was if the clouds knew to empty their bowels onto his life, turning it to crap. And it rained a lot in Panama City. That explained a lot about his life. It had been over half a year since he'd delivered the 15,000-pound load of marijuana to Katko, and he'd done a damn good job of distancing himself from Steinhorst. He'd been searching for a legitimate job down on the docks and at the local factories. He wasn't afraid of hard work because with it came a headache-free paycheck. There was a recession though, and no one was hiring. "Try back in a couple months. This will all pass," he was told time after time. But months had passed, and he still had not found a good job. He and his wife had used up the bankroll he'd received from the last drug deal; the last drug deal he thought he'd ever pull off. Now he was beyond desperate for cash.

With too much time on his hands, he became consumed with memories of the killing at the beach. And Ronnie Ray couldn't shake the thoughts of those two teenage girls whose friends and family had waited only to receive horrible news. So to escape the demons, he chose the worst possible remedy, and it came in bottles.

On the day Charlene had accepted his marriage proposal, she had made him take a solemn oath to never abuse booze or drugs. She had stayed with him through too many tribulations, and when he violated his oath night after night, Charlene's memories of an abusive alcoholic father returned. A few weeks ago, she'd left him and taken their son with her.

Ronnie Ray had lost almost twenty-five pounds over the summer and his once well-tanned body was beginning to look more like that of a big-city accountant than someone living along the gulf with a surfboard.

Like the old saying about criminals returning to the scene of the crime, it's also true that drunks return to their old hangouts. Tonight, Ronnie Ray took his last ten-dollar bill along to his favorite bar and stepped in out of the pouring rain. He had no reason to go home, which now was a dilapidated trailer by the beach. He clasped a bottle of ice-cold beer in both hands, determined to enjoy as many of these as he could afford tonight before financial reality kicked him in the ass tomorrow. He hadn't been there ten minutes before someone slid a chair next to him; the face was immediately familiar.

"Ronnie Ray, how you been?" the man asked, tossing back a shot of whiskey.

"Stevie Thomas? When the hell did you get out of the joint?"

"Been almost a year since I left the country club. Spent three damn years there, all expenses paid courtesy of the state. Three meals a day and a nice hard mattress," he chuckled. "Been in Memphis since I got out. Just got into town yesterday. How's it goin' bro?"

The two talked. Stevie bought Ronnie Ray a few more beers for old times' sake, and the night bled into morning. "It's tough finding a job around here," Ronnie Ray warned him. The condensation from his can of cold beer felt suddenly chilling.

"Damn. You know there's no way you're gonna punch a damn time clock at some plant. I ain't. Already found a good job, and it pays a hell of a lot more than anything you'll find on the docks. That's why I came back."

Ronnie Ray's curiosity was cautiously awakened. "Yeah?"

"Yeah, and we need one more guy. Money's great, and there's not much risk. Interested?"

The fact that his friend had to mention *not much risk* should have been a clue, but Ronnie Ray was desperate enough—and drunk enough—that he convinced himself there was no problem. "Definitely interested. What is it?" he asked in a thickly slurred voice.

Stevie leaned in. "Here's the sweet deal. We can make maybe a hundred thou for one night's work. Each. It's a once-in-a-lifetime score."

"A hundred thousand! What are we doing? Knocking off an armored car?"

"Just as good but without the risk. There's this chain of stores that sells cheap stuff. See, the managers of each store drop the cash bags at this central location where the money gets counted and put in bank bags. Then after the cash is counted, one of the managers takes it to a bank. He's only got one old security guard who can't even see, who goes with him to drop the cash deposit bags at the bank. One of my buddies has worked at one of those stores for ten years now, so he knows every detail. At the end of the route, the guard and manager take all the cash to a bank for deposit. Sunday is the biggest haul, and the guard picks up half a mil by the end of the night, and that's when we could rob the whole bundle of cash."

"I appreciate it, but I have a lead on a job. Hoping that will be enough for Charlene to take me back."

"Ok. Well, at least tell me you'll think about it."

RONNIE RAY DID. For two days he stayed in his trailer drinking. Then there was a knock on the door. It was Stevie Thomas. Ronnie Ray thought he was going to ask if he'd changed his mind, but instead, Stevie invited him to go out, and Stevie was buying. He wanted to bounce ideas around with Ronnie Ray to make sure every angle had been considered to pull off the robbery. And by the end of the night, Ronnie Ray, in a drunken stupor, had agreed to join him in the heist.

Stevie's friend, Lee, would be with them when they grabbed the cash. There was a guy on the inside who had planned the whole thing, and they'd never meet him. Only Lee knew his name. They'd split the money four ways.

Ronnie Ray met Lee for the first time a few days before the heist. They had some beers together and discussed details of the robbery. Then the actual day arrived.

First on Stevie's agenda was to steal a car so no one could link their name to the vehicle if it was identified during the heist. "It's a resort town, and we need to blend in. So let's look for a station wagon or a family van. Those vehicles would be less identifiable," Stevie said, as they inched through the parking lot of a motel near the beach, slowing down and craning his neck to peer at a few vehicles.

The only concern was someone catching them hot-wiring a vehicle, but they were ready to get out of there fast. They spotted several cars fitting the bill and tried the doors until they found one that was unlocked. As luck would have it, the owner of this Oldsmobile had "hidden" the keys in the visor, so in less than a minute, they were rumbling down a street headed away from the motel. If their luck held out, no one would notice the car missing until the next morning when they had their cash in hand and had already ditched the getaway car. Just to be safe, they pulled over and muddied the license plates so they were unreadable. Then it was time to park the car a few blocks away from their targeted store.

JUST AFTER DARK, the van driven by a lone security guard rolled along a block ahead of Ronnie Ray who had just pulled out of the parking lot and was keeping a safe distance. Stevie sat passenger, and Lee was in the back seat, both ready with their 9mm handguns. When the van pulled into the last pickup location, and the guard was inside the building, Ronnie Ray maneuvered the car into position where it was momentarily out of sight. When the guard and a manager came back out, Ronnie Ray careened around the corner of the building and sped up next to the van, taking the guard by surprise. He hadn't come to a full stop before Stevie and Lee were out of the car, Stevie's handgun was raised so it could be seen. They got the jump on the manager and elderly security guard. They grabbed the guard's handgun and the money bags then swiftly headed to the car.

It was at that point that the "no risk" deal crumbled. Several loud explosions cracked into the air behind them. They did not realize that the guard had a backup handgun. Ronnie Ray watched in panic as Lee tried to jump into the backseat, but a bullet pierced his head, taking a portion of it off that landed on the backseat. His body crumpled onto the pavement. Stevie ran, then stumbled and fell, scrambling to get back to the car. As soon as he jumped in through the open door, Ronnie Ray hit the accelerator, and they peeled away to the fading sound of more gunfire.

CHAPTER
TWENTY-TWO

FLORIDA
Fall 1977

RONNIE RAY SLEPT FITFULLY, tossing and startling awake throughout the entire night. He tried calling Stevie multiple times from a pay phone to no avail. As he put distance between himself and the crime scene last night, he heard sirens blaring that shook him from his semi-lucid slumber.

It was the relentless barking of the neighbor's German shepherd that first caused him to stir from a nightmarish slumber. The barking had become such an annoyance that he and his neighbor no longer spoke. At least not civilly. As congenial as Ronnie Ray was, he didn't let people trample on him, so he'd asked the lady to keep her dog quiet since he and others wanted to sleep past six in the morning.

"He has a mind of his own," she'd shrugged proudly. "When he decides to go outside and bark, he goes out." Since then, she'd been impossible to live next to.

Now the memories of the previous night were starting to light up in his brain, awakened by the morning sunlight creeping through faded curtains hanging from an angle on the window. Through the increasingly loud yapping of the dog, he heard a muffled announcement: "Ronnie Ray, this is the Panama City Police. Throw out your weapons and come out with your hands on your head!"

In one brief second, he went from tired and hungover to hyper alert. In fact, had he been of the mind to be paying attention, he could have declared a scientific breakthrough—a cure for the common hangover. Instead, wishful thoughts vibrated through his brain. Maybe they were here for some long-forgotten parking tickets he had stuffed in the glove box of the car. It couldn't be from last night; it had just happened. Maybe there was another Ronnie Ray who lived in the trailer park. All of the ridiculous hopes running through his mind couldn't push aside the reality of the situation. He peered through the window to find five heavily armed police officers standing behind patrol cars. One of the officers was holding a bullhorn and continued to demand "for the last time" that Ronnie Ray present himself before they stormed his trailer.

His stomach knotted as he found himself face down on the street, hands cuffed behind his back. When the police stood Ronnie Ray up, he heard a woman shout, "I knew he was no good! Just look at him. We're all lucky he didn't kill some of us!" It was the owner of the German shepherd.

On the way to the police station, Ronnie Ray sat silently in the back of the squad car. Finally one of the officers turned to him and said, "I'm surprised you didn't ask how we found you so quickly." Ronnie Ray didn't respond, and in a classic moment of law enforcement history, the officer decided to tell him. "Remember the friend you left at the scene with half of his damn head blown off? He had a slip of paper in his pocket that gave us the turn-by-turn directions to your trailer!" The two cops shared a dark laugh for a moment.

Ronnie Ray thought back to the previous night when he and Stevie had cleaned up the car, ditched it, and headed back to Stevie's where they'd split up the cash. The only positive thought was that he could use the money he'd stashed behind the paneling of his bedroom to get a good lawyer. "Yeah, your dead friend couldn't have been more cooperative. Unless of course he'd stayed alive and testified against you." The police radio crackled, and their attention was turned to the radio operator's question. Ronnie Ray sat wordlessly for the entire ride.

CHAPTER
TWENTY-THREE

FLORIDA
Fall 1977

THE DRAB GREEN walls of the conference room were closing in like a vice on Ronnie Ray. The charges filed against him included armed robbery, felony murder (because the guard shot and killed a man), and other assorted felonies the district attorney had managed to sandwich in for good measure, including threatening to seek the death penalty. The police had found the money hidden behind the paneling, and it was turned in as evidence. His court-appointed attorney was late, so now he had nothing to think about other than his uncontrollable leg jiggles and the deep shit he was in, facing life without parole in prison as a habitual criminal. Thirty minutes had passed that he'd spent sweating and chain smoking Winstons. His only hope was that this attorney turned out to be a good one with a plan for a reduced sentence. Ronnie Ray's entire future would rest in the hands of whoever this turned out to be.

Finally, the door creaked open and in strutted a tall thin black man. But what caught Ronnie Ray's attention was the man's afro, which was dyed a bright red.

"Who the *hell* are you?" Ronnie Ray blurted out, rising to his feet defensively.

The man flashed a wide smile and extended his right hand to Ronnie Ray. "I'm Earl Simpson, your court-appointed attorney."

"What's with the red hair, man?" he asked, unable to take his eyes off Earl's fire engine red head.

"Oh, that," the attorney said, running a hand through his thick afro and chuckling. "Yeah, I lost a bet with a friend, so I have to wear my hair red like this for three months."

Ronnie Ray let out a loud slow breath and shook his head. "This ain't good, dude. You look like a clown. I got heavy charges on me. This is my *life*! This court date is important to me."

Earl nodded in agreement while opening a leather briefcase he'd set on the table. Then he looked up with serious eyes. "Hey, it's important to me too! This is my first big case," he said, intending to sound comforting but having the opposite effect on Ronnie Ray who sat down, put his head in his hands and swore.

"You've damn well got to be kidding me," Ronnie Ray said flatly.

Earl explained the charges were very serious, especially the fact that a death occurred during an armed robbery.

"But I didn't kill no one," Ronnie Ray said meekly.

"Not a point of concern for the D.A. It's felony murder. You know how it is, Ronnie Ray. D.A.s do their D.A. thing." Earl ended by enthusiastically assuring Ronnie Ray that he would try everything in his power to bring justice to these charges.

Ronnie Ray was moved by the lawyer's compassion even though he didn't feel very confident about his future court dates. The Florida panhandle, bordered by Georgia and Alabama, felt more like the Deep South more than it did a part of Florida. Racial tensions ran high. Many citizens prided themselves on being rednecks. Something about Earl's demeanor let Ronnie Ray know that he was on a mission to prove his capability. Perhaps it wasn't something he should have needed to do, but there was determination behind every word he uttered. When the two shook hands at the end of the meeting, there was a promising connection that passed between them. There was no racial tension in these four walls, but in the court system there could be.

———

A WEEK CREPT BY, followed by another. Ronnie Ray heard nothing from his red-haired attorney Earl. Soon it was three weeks, a month, and then two months passed. He started to wonder if Earl had died or moved away. The affinity he'd felt for the lawyer, the one who held Ronnie Ray's future in his hands, had evaporated. He'd all but given up hope when a jailer came to his cell unexpectedly and escorted him to a dingy conference room where Earl sat at a chipped and scratched-up wooden table. He wore the same wide grin he'd had the first time.

Ronnie Ray came to a full stop. He was seething with anger toward the young attorney who'd left him high and dry for months. "*Where the hell you been? I've been sittin' in the stinkin' jail cell waitin' to hear word from yer lazy ass.*"

Earl's smile didn't fade. "Settle down. I've been working on your case, and I have good news! The D.A. has agreed to a plea deal. He is willing to accept thirty-five years. And remember that it could be even less with good time credit if you follow the rules in prison."

Ronnie Ray felt his muscles turn to lead as the reality sunk in. He stared straight ahead. He spoke slowly through thick lips. "Look, Earl. I know you tried, but just let me be. Let me think about some stuff, and I'll get back to you."

Earl nodded glumly, picked up his briefcase, and left feeling thwarted. It was not the reaction he'd expected from Ronnie Ray.

———

RONNIE RAY LAY on the thin mattress atop a hard metal frame, staring at the water-stained ceiling of his county jail cell. The same thoughts kept rolling through his brain:

I got two ways out of this thing. I can string myself up from the cell bars and check out of this life, or I can give 'em the biggest case they ever dealt with if they can give me something to live for.

Three days later, he met with the head jailer. "Get ahold of the Panama City Police. I got some information they're gonna want."

Only time would tell if he'd made the right decision.

WHEN TWO PANAMA CITY detectives came, Ronnie Ray wasted no time getting to the point. He'd rehearsed it in his head a thousand times, even in his sleep. He was ready to give all the information he had about the drug ring, but wouldn't say anything about the four murders at this time. That information might come in helpful later on. And, Steinhorst had threatened to kill anyone who spilled, so what was the point in getting out only to wind up dead.

He spoke hesitantly at first, practically whispering. "If I give you the biggest drug smuggling operation in the country, I'm gonna want a hell of a deal. I mean, this is big. Really, really big. Maybe about a billion dollars a year operation or something?" It came out like a question.

The detectives scribbled some notes on their pads. "Tell me more."

"They got boats, shrimp boats, warehouses, tractor trailers. These guys go from Texas to Georgia, Tennessee, New Jersey, and New York. I mean...it's huge." The detective continued writing briskly. Ronnie Ray dropped a few names including Charles Katko from New Jersey and a guy named Hawkins who owned a horse ranch in Texas. The detectives asked more questions, got more names, and told Ronnie Ray they'd make some calls and check things out.

"If what you're telling us is true, something should come up in the computer system, and we may need to call in the feds. If nothing comes up..." One of the detectives shrugged in a way that indicated Ronnie Ray probably wouldn't hear from him again.

The detectives made a call to a DEA agent they knew, Eugene Nance, who ran the names through NADDIS. Curiously, some names Ronnie Ray dropped matched up with an already open DEA case in New York.

CHAPTER
TWENTY-FOUR

FLORIDA
Fall 1977

SPECIAL AGENT BOFF worked with many extremely intelligent men. Several had graduated from Ivy League colleges at the top of their class. A handful of these intellectuals, however, walked on the eccentric side. One Assistant Special Agent in Charge, who supervised thirty to forty agents, had a foot-germ issue. Every day the ASAIC could be found sitting on the counter in the men's restroom scrubbing his feet in the sink. About midmorning he'd start thinking his feet were growing too many germs and had to be sanitized. And, as every agent knew, it was unwise to enter a bathroom when it was being used by the germaphobe. Venture in and you did so at your own risk. Once inside, the Assistant Special Agent in Charge would view you as either a pervert for being in a secluded room with another man or he'd hold you captive while he told war stories about all the defendants he had shot, beaten, or tortured during his thirty-year career.

Another unusual individual was Eugene Nance, who was not your typical Special Agent. A former coworker of Fred's in New York, he had relocated to Florida some years back partly due to his new wife who was from Florida, and also because of an unfortunate incident in a courtroom that had caused a lot of the government's hard work to go down the drain. Nance, or as some called him, "The Duck," due to his tendency to frequently talk in a Donald Duck voice, was eternally optimistic and had quickly adjusted to his new position within the Tallahassee DEA.

It was there that he received a call from a detective in Panama City regarding Ronnie Ray. "We have a three-time loser locked up here who says he might want to cooperate. The guy gave a few names to see if you'd be interested."

The names were Charles Katko, Carlos Gerdes, Walter Steinhorst, and David Goodwin among others. Nance listened to Ronnie Ray's claims as told to him by the cop and had his group supervisor in Tallahassee check the names through NADDIS. He was a bit surprised that most of the names turned up in an active file already in place in New York. Then Nance asked the GS to find out the name of the case agent in charge. It turned out to be the person who had the names entered into NADDIS the day after Thanksgiving.

"The Special Agent is Fred Boff. Ever heard of him?" the GS asked Nance.

CHAPTER
TWENTY-FIVE

NEW YORK
Winter 1977

FRED HATED New York during the unpleasant seasons. The English language doesn't include a word to describe his attitude toward having to navigate through the sloppy winter streets he shared with drivers who operated under the assumption that the best way to get to their destination was to do so dangerously fast. Instead of the leisurely twenty-eight-mile trip from the suburbs, which normally took him an hour, the winter weather tacked on an extra forty-five minutes. Not only that, but he was guaranteed at least one minor fender bender every year.

At 10:45 a.m., he finally walked into Group 5 only to discover that almost everyone else was either late or sick. Not surprising since the Channel 4 weatherman was predicting another five to six inches of snow on top of what was already piling up. If that happened, he'd just stay in the office and complete some overdue paperwork. The snow was picking up speed now and coming down in pellets. By 8:00 that night the roads would be cleared off, and he'd be able to head home.

Fred went up in the elevator, then slid his access card in the slot to unlock the office's door. He walked down the hall and could hear

Hatch, as dependable as a rooster, and the unmistakable laugh of Special Agent Redden. He couldn't make out their muffled conversation, but it sounded like they were sharing some camaraderie before digging into the day's work.

Fred reminded Hatch about some paperwork that had to be filled out. It was unusual since Hatch usually had his done the night before, while Fred handed his in at the last minute. The mundane weekly report was time-consuming with tiresome questions, such as the beginning and ending number of their odometer, and a place to staple receipts and whatnot. But the primary purpose was the daily allocation of man-hours expended by each agent and how much they'd worked on each case. Hatch came to his desk, grabbed the form, and started to leave. "Where ya going?" Fred asked, assuming they'd fill out the forms together and get them handed in right away.

"To check my odometer."

"You're kidding, right? You check your odometer every time you get out of your car. It's freezing out there. And snowing. And the garage is two blocks away. And we a have a thousand things to get done today."

Hatch's serious expression didn't falter. "That's what they want." He made a fifteen-minute trip to check the odometer, and when he returned Fred's form was nearly complete. Not accurate but complete since Fred considered it BS. For the beginning odometer number Fred had written "2" and for the ending number "200,002." It would get kicked back to him, but it was worth it just to mess with the pencil pushers.

Hatch came back shaking snow off his coat then fumbled through his wallet before producing a receipt he placed squarely in the stack with the others. Fred picked up the receipt. "This is for two bucks?" The statement came out as a question.

"It's a legitimate business expense. Film for the investigation. We're supposed to gather all relevant receipts to turn in. That's what they want."

Fred shook his head, being one to not bother even getting a receipt unless it was for an amount significant enough to count.

"Hey, after a month that kind of stuff adds up to some real money.

You might get a few bucks back in reimbursements." Hatch grabbed his forms and receipts and headed to his own office space to work in peace.

But then a few minutes later, Hatch was back poking his head into Fred's office. "You will *never* believe who's on the phone. All the way from Panama City."

Fred shook his head and shrugged.

"Come on! Take a guess."

"I don't care who it is, but if it's someone calling to break our balls about Florida's bright sunny weather in the mid-eighties, I don't want to hear about it." He returned to the task of filling out paperwork.

"No, no. It's an old friend. Just pick up the phone."

Although he felt he was being set up for one of Hatch's jokes, Fred did pick up. "Agent Fred Boff," he said reluctantly, keeping his eyes on Hatch.

Then loud quacking resounded from the receiver.

"Mr. Duck!" Fred said joyfully. "To what do I owe this phone call? You couldn't think of anyone else to harass about your warm weather?"

With that, the sound on the other end mutated into a human voice. It was Eugene Nance calling from Panama City. "My man, Fred. I hear you're a field supervisor now and still battling the jerks who run the place."

They discussed old times they had back in New York's Group 62 when the divisions were identified by two-digit numbers in multiples of ten such as ten, twenty, thirty, and forty. The groups in each division became eleven through thirteen or twenty-one through twenty-three, and so on. It was a simple system, so naturally a higher-up had to change it, and the groups became one, two, three, four, and so on. Fred's two years in Group 62 were among his favorites, and much of that fun was a direct result of Nance's colorful personality.

Nance had been on the path to becoming a priest and was close to becoming ordained when he changed his mind and became a Special Agent. It was something Fred had seen a handful of times. Agents he'd known had moved from a religious position to the DEA or from the DEA to a religious position, which solidified his belief that this job was as much a calling as anything. Not only did Nance come from an enormously wealthy Boston family with ties to the Kennedys, but he was one of the most entertaining people on earth who also kept the agents at ease. In the often traumatizing world of the DEA, such levity was essential. During those years, Fred had only seen him totally lose his composure once, and in that case the entire courtroom was witness to Nance's alter ego—Donald Duck.

The unfortunate episode had occurred in the midst of a massive trial regarding a conspiracy case that Fred had developed through a wiretap of cocaine dealers. Nance was working undercover, so his testimony was critical to winning the case. For the first few days, he held up well under grueling cross-examination by a team of top-notch defense attorneys. Then one of them attacked not only Nance's credibility but his integrity. He was pushed to his tipping point. As everyone in the office knew, Nance held his integrity in high regard, coming from an old-world Boston family. He would never compromise his career for a bribe of a few thousand measly dollars as suggested by the attorney—or for any amount.

The strain began showing on Nance's face. First, the beads of sweat popped out on his forehead, next he reached inside the rear of his collar and grabbed the top of his t-shirt and began pulling it, a habit that apparently brought him a sense of security. Fred knew it was only a matter of time, but he was powerless to change the course of action now. The problem with Nance's method of security was that it never stopped with a small tug; he continued to twist the fabric around and around his finger pulling out more of the cotton t-shirt until a foot-long strand twirled before him. The judge did a double-take, and Fred got up and warned the assistant U.S. attorney in charge of the case that things could get strange. "This could get damn ugly," Fred told him quietly. Then he walked to the door to leave. He had no intention of getting caught in the middle of what was about to occur.

It was too late. Nance totally lost it. Loud, rapid quacking erupted from deep within his lungs and filled the room. There in front of the astonished judge, teams of attorneys, and a courtroom full of spectators sat Special Agent Eugene Nance flailing his arms up and down like an angry duck. Then *"quack, quack, quack"* again. Everyone sat in stunned silence as the agent became more agitated, quacking faster and louder and yanking on his t-shirt relentlessly. If anyone in the room had closed their eyes, they would have thought Donald Duck himself was right there. He was quacking yet speaking coherently in this cartoon voice. Finally, the judge had the decency to order a recess.

In the hall, Fred had just stepped into the elevator when prosecutor Michael Mukasey came up to him breathlessly. "What the hell was that? Is he effing crazy?" he steamed.

"He's not crazy," Fred said. "He's a duck trapped in a man's body."

"A *duck*?" The prosecutor leaned forward as if waiting for more information.

Fred wasn't sure what else to say. Nance truly, during times of stress, thought he was a duck. Nance kept four porcelain figurine ducks on his desk and claimed they were his family. One day Nance got into an argument with a fellow agent who in anger reached over and smashed one of the porcelain ducks before storming out of the office. Nance's wails of horror could be heard throughout the office. For days he'd sulked around in a state of depression until Fred finally asked, "What's wrong with you?"

Pointing to the office of the agent who broke the porcelain duck, Nance replied in a weak, shaky voice, "He *killed* one of my family members!"

"You've got to be kidding," Fred replied, truly dumbstruck. "It was a figurine!"

But to Nance it wasn't, and choosing his words carefully, Fred attempted to explain the situation in the courtroom to the judge later that day. Nance truly believed he was a duck trapped in a man's body. Underneath it all, he was a good person.

The prosecutor leaned forward. "And they gave this guy a gun?" he responded incredulously.

Needless to say, the rest of the trial did not go well for the government. Just before the closing statements, the U.S. Attorney's office offered a deal that couldn't be refused. The defendants accepted a deeply reduced sentence of five years each rather than the fifteen the feds had been hoping for. Several months later, The Duck was on his way to Florida. If it hadn't been for Fred and a few other agents, Nance would have been living in Boston and working a desk job at one of his family's investment banking offices.

Now on the other end of the phone, Fred listened as Nance suggested that agents from New York come down to interview Ronnie Ray and figure out the connection to the case that was already open. Fred agreed and had ulterior motives: weather! He looked outside at all the snow that had fallen the day before and couldn't think of anywhere he'd rather be than far away from it.

"We're taking a little trip down south," Fred cheerfully explained to Hatch. "We'll be interviewing an informant by the name of Ronnie Ray."

A DAY LATER, the men could see the New York City skyline growing smaller as they rose higher into the air leaving Newark Airport behind them.

"Go ahead," Fred said and motioned for Hatch to start talking.

"Go ahead with what?"

"Whatever you're going to say. 'The wing looks loose. The pilot looked a little drunk when we got on.' All that shit you know I hate. Go ahead and get it over with."

Hatch shrugged one shoulder. "Not this time."

Fred hated flying. "You know if I get on a plane there's a good reason. Like now. We deserve a little southern vacation after pulling late nights in the Village for a year straight, right?"

Hatch looked slightly puzzled. "Well, we'll be interviewing—what's his name, Ronnie Ray—in a dank room of a rinky-dink jail, if you call that a vacation."

Fred laughed deviously and nodded knowingly, taunting Hatch with an I-know-something-you-don't-know approach until Hatch finally gave in.

"Ok, what's so funny? I guess I don't get it."

"Did I really convince you that there's some guy named Ronnie Ray who just happens to be located near the warm sunny waters of Panama City Beach?" He leaned forward with laughter and slapped

Hatch on the knee. Hatch went rigid and the smile drained from his face.

"Are you bullshitting me?" His voice had an edge of desperation.

Fred started up with his most fiendish laughter. "Damn, Hatch, if the higher-ups can use government money for lavish vacations under the pretense of 'investigation,' so can we! This whole trip is a scam, and no one will ever know that."

"This is not funny, Fred." Hatch's voice went up a level. "We can't do this. We could be fired. And if we don't get fired, it's completely unethical. Damn. It's not worth it for a few days of fun in Florida. Ah-and, and...you *hate* flying!"

Hatch couldn't stop himself. For the next hour he fumed that he was going to "use my own money to pay for the cheapest motel I can find and take a bus if that's what I have to do to get back to New York."

"Don't worry. I covered it up. No one will know," Fred said unconcerned.

Hatch's face had gone red all the way to his ears, and when he appeared close to hyperventilating and managed to spit out, with a total lack of empathy, that when "you lose your job, don't come crawling to me for help!" Fred finally came clean.

"Oh, don't come to my former best friend for help?" he said with faux anger. "Fine! I won't because...well, I have been bullshitting you. There really is a Ronnie Ray, so relax and get ready to enjoy some sun!" He erupted into more laughter. "Do you really think I'd pull a stunt like that when I'm with 'Hatch the Righteous,' king of following every regulation ever written?"

Hatch scowled and threw a wadded-up napkin that bounced off the side of Fred's face. "I knew you were bullshitting," Hatch said, clearly irritated that he'd been the butt of another Fred joke. In due time he'd get Fred back with his own prank.

CHAPTER
TWENTY-SIX

FLORIDA
December 1977

A FEW HOURS LATER, they stepped from the terminal and breathed in the humid Florida air. The ladies in the travel office had booked them what was considered standard economical hotel accommodations for this type of case—something along the lines of what travelers referred to as a cheap hotel. The low-budget per diem rate the agents received had to include their hotel, meals, and incidentals. "We'll get a rental car and then go see this Ronnie Ray in the morning," Fred commented, and Hatch nodded in agreement.

They headed to the poolside bar. It was one of those modern fiberglass creations with a sagging straw roof made from polyester strands of grass. Nance was there with two Panama City police officers; they'd made plans to go over all the information and had spread several bulging folders on the table before them.

"Let's not get carried away," Fred cautioned. "It's only 4:00, and I haven't even had a drink yet." He had a method to his madness. The strength of the investigation would hinge on the strength of the trust between the different agencies. DEA agents didn't give away their trust easily; one thing they rarely shared was specific names. They were trained not to trust anyone except other agents. Even that was on a need-to-know basis. There was a lot of legitimate paranoia. One group supervisor was referred to as Whispering Pines because anytime he shared privileged information he whispered it in case the room was bugged. Ginger had once put her hands on her hips and announced, "You don't trust me," to which Fred had simply replied, "I don't." He'd been trained not to share delicate information with anyone since it was too easy for someone to slip up with information that could result in lives being put in danger.

DEA agents lived with the fear of being hurt or killed. It was part of the job, so they learned to live with it. Many days were spent in contact with some of the most ruthless people on earth. Add in the amount of money at stake and prison time some of these people faced, and it created a state of desperation that made them capable of anything. While Fred feared for his own life, it didn't compare to the worries he had about his own family. While retaliation against spouses and children was rare, it didn't allay the fear. The DEA was also very guarded about the identification of informants and witnesses. Without trust, information is rarely shared. So the drinking and bullshitting that went on throughout the night had a much more significant purpose and would pay off in the days—or weeks—ahead.

The five of them headed to a seafood restaurant and ordered clams, shrimp, and lobster for a bit of camaraderie at the government's expense. They left intending to go back to the hotel and organize their notes. As fate would have it, they passed a bar and went in for one last beer. And then another. And then they went back to the pool by the hotel where one of the police officers pulled out a glass bottle of whiskey-colored liquid.

And the dark night turned black....

━━━

FRED'S ALARM went off at 8:30 a.m. He hit the snooze repeatedly until Hatch came to fetch him at 10:00. By the time they got to the hotel restaurant, Nance and both policemen were already there.

"Tough night for the boys from New York?" one of them asked.

"Tough night? Crap. I feel like I got hit on the head with a baseball bat. What was that stuff?"

"That, my friend, was the best homemade whiskey in the entire country. My Uncle Will's been making it for forty years. He claims it's 190 proof and says that if you aren't man enough to drink it, you can use it as an industrial cleaner instead. Great, isn't it?" The officer's voice was cheerful, but the bags under his eyes told a different story.

"Homemade? You mean the stuff cooked up in bathtubs that makes people go blind? That poison could've killed us."

"Eh. Can you still see?"

When the waiter came, Fred ordered eggs and sausage with a large glass of milk to settle his stomach, which felt as if it had been stripped raw by varnish. It didn't work, and thirty minutes later he was leaning over a bathroom toilet bemoaning his fate.

After another hour of attempting to lift their physical condition to a functioning level, they finally got on their way to the Bay County dungeon for a face-to-face with Ronnie Ray.

It was a tough morning after, but the previous night proved to Hatch and Fred that they'd have no problem working closely with the Panama City police officers.

Fred and Hatch eased themselves into plastic chairs that groaned beneath their weight. They sat in a conference room sipping black coffee from Styrofoam cups and waited for the jailer to bring Ronnie Ray; the coffee was a must-have drink that went with the job, especially on a morning like this. The door creaked open to reveal the agents' first look at the perp they'd be interviewing. Not a small guy, Ronnie Ray stood six-foot-two and was nearly two hundred pounds. His hair and teeth were the product of neglect, and the first thought to cross their minds was *trailer trash*. When Ronnie Ray spoke, their initial impressions were confirmed. Ronnie Ray took a seat across from Fred who noticed the man's movements were both awkward, yet had an almost child-like flourish. There was something about Ronnie Ray that made him appear harmless.

After introductions, Fred began. "First, everything you tell us has to be the truth to the best of your knowledge. If you're not sure of something, tell us. If we catch you lying about anything, the deal's off. Do you understand?"

"Yeah, I know all that," Ronnie Ray responded, unsurprisingly familiar with the ins and outs of being questioned and cooperating. Even so, he was shifting uncomfortably in his chair.

"Hence, we can't guarantee—"

"Hen…hence? Who?" Ronnie Ray appeared unduly confused.

"I'm just saying that we can't guarantee you anything or tell you you'll walk away from the state charges. But if your cooperation helps us take down some of these people, we'll write to the judge and prosecutor about your assistance—about your help. The U.S. Attorney's Office will help you out as well. In the end, it's still all up to the prosecutor and judge, but if you do right by us, it should help when we go to bat for you. Also, we'll try to get you out of here, but you already have two felonies on your record. What you're facing now in Florida is three strikes, which makes you habitual, and that's life behind bars."

"Wait! You might get me out of here?" Coming from a typical felon, the question could have come across as too eager; a chance to skip out of town. But Ronnie Ray sounded genuinely touched, as though in awe that anyone might think to get him out of jail.

"Might. And if we get you out of this shithole jail, and you run on us, you will get caught, and there will never be a chance for another deal. You will go bye-bye for life. Got it?" Fred asked sternly.

"I got it," Ronnie Ray said humbly. He sat with his head bowed and picked at a fingernail for the rest of the interview, during which he provided more and more details, beginning with the load of marijuana that had arrived on the *Gunsmoke*. Suddenly, he couldn't tell them fast enough. In a rush of words he lit into a fiery retelling of that disastrous night in Sandy Creek.

"What kind of boats did they use to ferry the marijuana to shore?" Fred asked.

"Them luma…luna…lunamin boats. There were three of 'em."

"Three aluminum boats?"

"Yeah. That's it. They was fourteen footers. Vines told me."

"Vines?"

"Bobby Vines. He owned the boats."

It was a long interview, and at the end, Fred shook his hand. Ronnie Ray reciprocated with more confidence than he'd had at the start of the interview. The deal was in motion, but both agents suspected Ronnie Ray had a lot more to say. Cons never gave up all their good info during the first interview. They were certain he'd kept an ace up his sleeve.

That night, Fred revealed his suspicions to the police officers, and to Hatch, along with Redden who'd arrived after them. It was during another long night over strong drinks that Redden gave them a further glimpse into his background. He opened up a little every time he segued from sober to the nether regions, which lately had been often.

"The reason my shoes are always in good condition," he slurred, "is because I appreciate them. When I was growing up—I'd say junior high because I was a big kid and grew fast—my mom couldn't afford to keep me in shoes. She cut the toes off my sneakers so my feet would fit." Redden had been a high school teacher and coach in Iowa and was diligent about making sure his athletes had decent shoes.

It had at first seemed somewhat humorous and brought forth a few snorts from the other agents.

"But let me tell you, being in junior high and showing up at school with the toes of my sneakers cut off was not ideal. Oh, I think I can remember every snicker and every joke. It's a mean age for kids, and I guess my size didn't help. At the time anyway. Then a few weeks later someone invited me to a birthday party, and I thought the tides had changed. Turns out they invited me just to make fun. I was looking forward to eating cake since once again we had no food in our house. But they'd invited me to see if I actually believed they wanted me there, which they didn't. So after they made fun of my raggedy clothes I went back home, cakeless, through slush and snow, with open-toed shoes. And that, gentlemen, is the story of why George Redden always wears nice shoes."

It was a story that sealed the deal for Fred. He'd taken an instant liking to George, who was humble despite having played football at a prestigious college and had a reputation as someone who could squeeze the truth out of the most notorious liar. Fred grew to respect this poor kid who worked his way to becoming a Special Agent by relying on his own fortitude.

The paperwork to get Ronnie Ray out of jail was being processed quickly. Once that happened, Ronnie Ray would be required to continue providing information, which meant they'd be in Florida for an extended period of time. This called for better accommodations, so they packed up their suitcases to head across town. Cars moved with the rashness of afternoon commuters, but the destination would be worth it. Fred had located a beautiful three-bedroom condo to rent. "The government has great taste in accommodations," Hatch noted on the shore of Panama City Beach where they decided to skip dinner and go straight to the drinks. They were going to be here awhile, and this was clearly grounds for procuring a better place to sleep and conduct business.

CHAPTER
TWENTY-SEVEN

FLORIDA
Winter 1977

RONNIE RAY HAD AWOKEN as a jailbird and gone to bed liberated, the door to his cage having been thrown open by the likes of three strangers—agents from New York. He was feeling pretty good. He was out of the stinking county jail (which was always too hot or too cold), sleeping in a condo on the beach, and eating great food. The food in jail had been the worst he'd ever eaten. He was able to call his son and give him the good news; he was not going to prison for life as Charlene had feared. Though no longer married, she encouraged Ronnie Ray to be a decent father. He would have to stay with these DEA agents for as long as it took to give them all the information they needed on the drug smuggling case, and he'd need to keep giving them good information. Often, this took a year at the minimum.

▭

"I RAN drugs up to Jersey to a guy named Katko," he said, outlining details on where the marijuana was stored, where Katko kept the marijuana, and how he sold it in increments of one thousand pounds. "The pot comes in, like…I dunno, maybe every month or something from Colombia. It comes on them shrimp boats. One boat is the *Agnes Pauline,* but we call her *Aggie.*"

"That's good information, Ronnie Ray. Those are the types of details we need," Fred said while he and Hatch continued taking notes. At this encouragement, Ronnie Ray sat taller and took on a glow of confidence.

"I drove some to Tennessee, and I been on deliveries to a ranch owned by a guy named Hawkins. This Hawkins has lots of money. And I also went on runs to Denton, Texas, to the ranch The Old Man owns," he continued, searching for those golden crumbs of information that would bring him more of Fred's fatherly praise. "Yeah, it's a hell of a spread. Out front of the place is a statue of a gold horse, and I seen like a rodeo ring there. They store the pot in big horse barns. It ain't hidden or nothing, just sittin' in there." He let out a deep sigh.

"Who's 'The Old Man'? What's his real name?"

"I don't know his real name. Everyone calls him The Old Man. I don't run to Texas much, but man he's *rich.*" Then, as if disappointed in himself for not being able to answer the question, he came up with another name. "Oh yeah, The Old Man owns the ranches, but the real top dog is a guy named Muscles. Seems like everyone reports to Muscles."

"And Muscles's real name is…?"

Again, Ronnie Ray didn't know, and he saw a flicker of disappointment in the agents' eyes. Something within him craved their approval, especially Fred's, and his brain finally landed on a way to make up for his lack of knowledge on some of the details they sought, but it would have to wait until tomorrow.

Fred and Hatch had the names and cities run through NADDIS, and Ronnie Ray's information started to line up. "He's checking out, and he's been honest. So far," Fred commented. He hadn't only asked Ronnie Ray about the drug operation but also about his background, where he grew up, and other details to see if all of his stories rang true and were consistent. When he discovered that Ronnie Ray had spent time living on the street, Fred thought back to his own childhood. His dad, a well-respected dentist, had found himself pulled into the clutches of gambling when Fred was a teenager. The family had almost lost their house, but Fred's uncles had pulled together and paid off the past-due mortgage debts. There'd been no family standing by Ronnie Ray's mom. *By the grace of God,* Fred thought. Many informants were dishonest antisocial criminals, and Ronnie Ray was clearly different. After only two days, Fred and Hatch had developed a fondness for the humble, soft-spoken informant; a rarity since neither agent was quick to trust.

The next morning, Hatch woke up and glanced out the front window of a three-bedroom condo. It was a well-ingrained habit of his to continually check his surroundings. An orange sky was spreading upward with the rising of the sun. But what caught his eye was that where last night had sat their car parked in its usual spot was now an empty space. Hatch's mouth went dry. A dizzying rush of blood rose in his head. He threw back the curtain and rushed into Fred's room, and there lay his partner, mouth open and sound asleep. Panic rose in his chest, and he ran on shaky legs to Ronnie Ray's room. Gone!

"Damn it! *Damn it!*" Hatch bellowed. "Fred, get the hell up! That worthless son of a bitch ran on us, and he took our car!" In the case of a near death, it is widely reported that one's life flashes before their eyes. Fred shot out of bed. Now, his career flashed before his eyes—first as a new recruit, then long hours away from his family, and the constant threat of danger. The red tape he often cursed suddenly didn't seem so bad as he envisioned all of it being abruptly snatched away from him when the higher-ups discovered that Ronnie Ray had disappeared. Typically, Fred was even-tempered, slow to anger, but at this moment he felt the veins pop out of his temples, and his body went hot. Hatch was throwing on a t-shirt and pants. Fred was hollering. It was an anger Hatch hadn't heard from his partner before.

"I signed for that two-faced snitch! My damn job is on the line now! I'm supposed to have him in federal jail in New York, and I have him down here in Florida 'living it up' in a damn condo! How's that going to look?"

Hatch shook his head. The two of them pondered their next moves, with Fred pacing from one end of the bedroom to the other. They'd need to borrow another Special Agent's car, drive around, check out some of Ronnie Ray's old haunts, his ex-wife...

At that moment, there was a sound in the front room; Hatch put a hand to his service revolver and bolted forward while Fred stood motionless in his boxers. Then they stopped short. It was an exuberant Ronnie Ray, forcing the door open with his elbow, his arms laden with waxed paper bags and cups of coffee.

Ronnie Ray smiled brightly and nodded to the bounty in his arms. "I brought donuts and—"

"You stupid sneaky son of a bitch!" Fred roared and his face reddened. He threw his shirt on the couch and took two strides toward Ronnie Ray with clenched fists. The veins in his neck pulsed. "You stole our damn car and ran off?" He let loose a string of curse words that he wasn't sure had ever left his mouth previously.

Ronnie Ray started stammering and went limp. "I... I didn't run... I didn't run off! I went out and got us donuts and coffee. The...the keys were on the t-table, so I just used the car. I thought about you and got your favorites—jelly donuts. Y-you'd mentioned last night that you like jelly donuts." Ronnie Ray turned white. He hesitantly set the donuts and coffees on a table and sat down, his legs having gone noodly.

Fred stood glaring and breathing in loud snorts through his nose while the rage billowed inside him. No one spoke. Finally Fred opened his mouth, and all he could utter was, *"Jelly donuts!"*

With each mouthful of sweet jelly donut, Fred's blood pressure lowered. He was sitting in boxer shorts on the side of his bed, thinking. Ronnie Ray knocked on the open door and asked to come in. "Can I talk to you now, Fred?"

Fred took another bite then pointed at a chair where Ronnie Ray could sit.

"Fred, you told me you'd take care of me, right?"

"If you're telling us the truth. If you're not, we'll find out, and you'll be facing life," Fred said in a changed tone.

With that reminder, Ronnie Ray's face lost the little color it had left after weeks in the jail. "I am tellin' you the truth... I just ain't found a way to…to tell you everything." Ronnie Ray hung his head and wrung his hands together.

"Well, let's hear it," Fred said impatiently.

Following a long pause, Ronnie Ray took a deep breath and began in a quiet voice. "One night we was unloading a shipment and two kids—two sisters—and two other dudes show up. They just drove up on us and…and got theirselves wacked and thrown in a sinkhole. I was there, but only because this crazy guy, Steinhorst, made me go with him. It was a nightmare for them people who got wacked, and for me since then. I didn't never want to be part of something like that. Just wanted some extra cash to help my family. It's been all over the news. People tryin' to figure out who did it, ya know. Then some divers found 'em at the bottom of the sinkhole."

Ronnie Ray had done some quick soul-searching before sharing this story. Steinhorst had threatened his life not once or twice but multiple times. In fact, he had made it a habit to make threatening phone calls to Ronnie Ray, Hughes, and others who knew what went down that night and remind them that they and their loved ones would never be safe if they spilled what they knew.

It weighed too heavily on Ronnie Ray, and, truth be told, if ever there was an opportunity for him to have a chance at getting out of those charges, now was the time. Just as importantly, whether he knew it or not at the time, he had an insatiable desire for approval from others. Ronnie Ray desperately needed someone he could trust and count on. Fred represented that type of a person in his life.

Fred wrote down the names and dates, including who pulled the trigger. "Anything else? Are there any other details you can think of? Sometimes the seemingly meaningless details end up being important. Remember, you don't know what information might be the key to reducing these charges against you."

There was a long pause during which time Ronnie Ray swallowed hard and seemed on the verge of saying something but then stopped. Fred waited patiently.

"Well, uh, just that…you know, I didn't know what was going to happen, and I told the girls everything would be okay. They'd be back home. You gotta believe me, I really thought that's what would happen." He hung his head in his hands, unable to go on. After a minute, he continued. "Right before those girls got shot, the one looked at me. She thought I'd betrayed her...she, well, what if her last thought on earth was she'd been betrayed, and it was my fault?"

Fred sat in stunned silence. *Dear God, this man actually has a conscience.* Ronnie Ray should have been focusing on what he could do to help his case but instead was concerned about what this girl thought of him before she died.

Fred got dressed and within twenty minutes had called Hatch, Nance, and the two Panama City police officers into an informal meeting. After discussing the murders, they decided to turn it over to the police department, since it would be a local or state crime rather than a federal one. Ronnie Ray then went on to share information about the murders with Panama City homicide detectives. Though the police had initially suspected that the Sandy Creek marijuana debacle was related to the four missing people, there had been no witness stepping forward until now.

Redden was the last to arrive at the pool later that night. Fred was sitting deep in thought until Hatch broke the silence. "And now we head back to New York to piece together as much as we can on this thing. Fred, this looks to be shaping up into something big. This is one crazy job we have."

Fred nodded. "Yeah, and who'd think a local mass murder would get solved while sitting in boxer shorts eating jelly donuts and drinking coffee." It dawned on him that Ronnie Ray didn't rub him the wrong way like most of the seedy informants he had to work with. The guy was actually easy to be around. When he wasn't taking off with Fred's car.

Later, one of the police officers who knew a bit about Ronnie Ray's mom, made some comments about her apparent lack of morals and how it was no surprise that her son had a rap sheet. Fred noticed a dark change in George Redden's demeanor. Fred knew there would be a story forthcoming that night.

"YOU DON'T KNOW why some women make the choices they do. But it's not the kid's fault." The words started to pour out several drinks into the evening.

"You grew up with just a mom, right?" Fred asked.

George nodded. "We were just a normal family until my dad fell off the roof of the barn and died. We lost everything after that. We were homeless. Relatives took us in occasionally. My mom did her best. I don't know. Maybe she didn't. We never had enough. Not enough food, clothes, you name it. I didn't put two and two together until I was in high school…"

Fred felt a knot in his stomach. George had endured such a hard life and yet was so understanding of others, when he could have been mean and judgmental.

"Whenever there was no food, I mean not even a crumb, I'd see her take off with a truck driver in his semi. It was a different guy every time. Even as a kid I noticed stuff like that. She'd come back with money, and we'd have food for a few days." His mouth quivered slightly, though whether it was from copious amounts of alcohol or gloom Fred wasn't sure. George uncapped a new bottle of whiskey and poured them both a stiff shot.

"A close relative told me in a not-so-kind manner one day what my mom was doing with all these men. I was in high school at the time and didn't believe it at first. Then it sank in. I thought back to the times she took us to a truck stop, talked to some random trucker, and left us there while she took off with some strange man for an hour. I lost all respect for her. I was determined to turn out different."

Fred pondered as his late-evening head began to spin in full force. "You know, my friend. There is another way to look at it. Remember those were the days when it was tough for a woman to find a job. From the sounds of it, your mom was willing to do whatever she had to for her kids to eat. If she hadn't, did she fear her kids would be taken away from her?" Shame settled over Fred. When the family had almost lost their house, they still had a home on the Jersey Shore. He'd been so concerned about having to live on the Jersey Shore when George had gone through so much worse.

George sat thinking. He nodded off for a few minutes and woke in a somewhat better state of mind.

"It was, in my opinion, one of the greatest sacrifices she could have made," Fred added.

George rested his elbows on his knees and put his head in hands. It was a moment that would define their friendship. Fred unwittingly became George's mentor and would advise him many times in years to come.

AS IT TURNED OUT, Fred's next opportunity to mentor George came the moment they stepped back into the bustle of the New York DEA building. They walked down a brightly lit hallway and turned into "Base"—the communication center where all calls and anonymous tips came in by phone after hours. It was located in the inner sanctuary of the building and had a single door and no windows. Fred had once been told it was due to a fear of someone being able to spy on the office. "Hey, paranoia runs deep," they'd said, to which Fred had replied with the old agent's saying that, "it ain't paranoia if they're really out to get you."

The room was large but painted drab white, and contained little other than some wall calendars and half a dozen radio operator stations, each with a radio and telephone. It was staffed twenty-four hours a day, usually by young government employees striving to become agents, as an important call could come in at any time. Fred heard that phone tips had come in related to Katko's associates, and he took George with him to see if there were any new developments.

Today, a group supervisor was on a phone call along with two others. One was a woman with long dark hair who was on the phone taking notes. Fred had met her before, a criminal justice major from a local college. "The FBI told you to call this number?" she replied while shaking her head. She turned to Fred and George and rolled her eyes.

Fred groaned. That was a sure sign of a pointless, wacky call. While many calls were legitimate tips, a good share were from irrational people with unbelievable stories. The woman taking notes motioned for Fred and George to come closer so they could hear the call.

"Could you repeat that?"

The phone crackled, and a frantic voice launched into a long, seemingly rational story. "I come home from work every day at 3:00. I use the elevator to get to my apartment on the fifth floor." The woman continued outlining a scene in which every step of her mundane trip home was as expected until she stepped into the elevator. "...and when I saw the hose, I followed it to a window which is where I discovered *Martians* pumping heroin gas into the apartment. My apartment!"

It had unwittingly become a joking game among the DEA, FBI, and NYPD. Sometimes the DEA received 100–200 tips per night, and the agents assigned to the center did twelve-hour shifts for seven straight days. Stress ran high. So when the tip lines were excessively busy, and a nutty call came in, the tip-taker would explain that this was definitely a problem the FBI, or NYPD (depending on the night), needed to handle. The zany caller would be given the phone number to one of the other agencies so they would have to field the worthless call. Of course, the FBI and NYPD did the same thing, so when a caller started out explaining that one of these agencies had directed them to call the tip line, the receiver of the call knew it would be a waste of time. But the credible tips were passed on to the proper enforcement group.

When the call wrapped up, the woman turned to Fred. "We've had a lot of calls tonight, what kind of tip are you looking for?" Her phone had already started ringing again. Fred explained what he needed, and shuffled through her pile of papers from the night while she took the next call. After a few minutes she wordlessly held up one of the intake forms and waved it back and forth while taking notes with her other hand.

Fred took the intelligence report. He and George anxiously scanned the information, which looked helpful. They were still tracking down dealers who bought marijuana from Katko. One of the required lines asked why the person was cooperating, and this one stated, "Concerned citizen." *Yeah, right.* More likely it was a drug-dealing competitor trying to get his rival arrested and off the street. Some informants made a nice living off of supplying information. Over the course of several years in the 1970s, Fred's group paid around $150,000 to Jack, a factory owner who regularly had leads on people in the drug business. But the reason why someone had supplied this information on Katko didn't matter. The information looked hopeful, so they took the information back to Fred's office to start investigating.

CHAPTER
TWENTY-EIGHT

NEW YORK
Winter 1977

IN THE MIDST of what was possibly the DEA's biggest drug case, the world did not slow down to let Fred focus solely on the immense job before him. The bosses continued to call regular meetings to address the day-to-day issues that cropped up. Today everyone was to be in the conference room at 9:00 a.m. Fred had to not only battle the heavy morning traffic but also had to reroute himself due to a fender bender in the road ahead.

He made it to the meeting just in time. One of the bosses walked up to the podium holding a clipboard thick with papers.

Fred leaned back in his chair scowling and whispered to Hatch and Redden, "I have a bad feeling about this crap, and we have more important things to focus on. Especially you, Redden."

Redden gave him a confused look and shrugged, "Me?"

"Yeah, I don't like seeing my idol wasting his time in meetings."

"*He's* your idol?" Hatch asked with faux indignation.

"Yeah, of course!" Fred said in his most serious voice. "I mean not because he has any special skills or talents as far as an agent, but what other guy pushing forty is dating a pretty twenty-three-year-old secretary?" He and Hatch burst into laughter, while Redden dramatically flexed his muscles and made some comment about his physical prowess.

The boss flipped through his papers and got right to the point. "Okay, men, listen up. Our friends out in Washington don't think we've been working hard enough. They want more results. They want more arrests." The boss shuffled from foot to foot knowing his words would cut deep into the men who put their lives on the line every day. "So, if we want our budget money, we've got to give them statistics, and that means drug arrests."

Even though the Special Agents were swamped with big cases, this was a situation they had to deal with at least one time a year. They had to appease the "Big Boys" in Washington.

Over the next two weeks, vital investigations were sidelined so they could go out on the streets and make arrests. But they were what the Special Agents called bullshit arrests. Some hippie guy smoking a single joint on a street corner: *Busted!* Two eighteen-year-old kids getting high in the park: *Busted!* Four Wall Street traders passing a joint around a picnic table at lunch: *Busted!* It was all bullshit.

The Assistant U.S. Attorney declined prosecution in the majority of the cases. The filed charges were dismissed, but these busts still counted to the micromanagers in Washington as drug enforcement statistical arrests. Due to the "war on drugs," the politicians wanted to have statistics to show success. More arrests would get the local office more manpower even if the arrests were low-level crimes that were eventually dismissed. Then having more manpower in the office increased the pay grade for the higher-ups. So, the top dogs pushed the frustrated agents to make more arrests. After two weeks of what Fred called a waste of taxpayers' money, he, Redden, and Hatch could finally go back to focusing on their real work in Florida, Texas, and a multitude of other locations.

Another stressful situation weighed heavily on Fred's mind. It was typical to have ten to fifteen cases open at one time, and now was no exception. Fred's group didn't have the luxury of focusing only on the ever-expanding operation Ronnie Ray had led them to. Fred and Ginger had never experienced marital problems, but the other day she sat him down when he arrived home after a fourteen-hour day.

"You're a hard worker, but I can't do this anymore, Fred. I didn't sign up to be a single parent."

Fred's head dropped in despair. "Ginger, honey, things will slow down. Drug dealers don't just wait around while I take a day off," he joked. He scooted closer to Ginger on the couch and put his arm around her.

"Please stop. I'm serious, Fred. Your kids are growing up without a dad in the house. They see you for five minutes in the morning, and then you're not back until they're in bed. Or they don't see you for a week."

Fred's heart sank. Every day he tried to focus on how he was making the country a safer place for his family. But at what cost? He searched for the right words, but none appeared on his tongue.

"It's been ten months, Fred. Ten months of working seven days a week. Let that sink in. The entire time David was a baby, you weren't here."

Ginger laid it on thick. His job had always been demanding, but had nearly spiraled out of control during the *Hermit* case in the spring of 1976 when Fred had been heavily involved in investigating a hash-smuggling ring. At the time he'd been at it seven days a week for three straight months and felt like a gambler chasing the big payoff. *Next time we'll catch that sailboat the Hermit,* he'd think in the same way an addict would keep feeding a slot machine, rationalizing that it was time to hit the jackpot. He had paused just long enough to make a call home. "Daddy, when will I see you?" It was a question that tore at the scab on his heart every time three-year-old Suzie asked it. And she'd had to ask too many times lately. Fred looked at the date on the newspaper spread before him then began counting back each day. It had been a long time since he'd taken a break. He was working a few different cases. "I'll be home in three days, Suzie. I miss you so much."

"Will you take me to the shore?"

Fred paused. There was so much he needed to get done, but he'd promised Ginger that he was determined to make more time for his family.

"Sure! I'll take you to the Jersey Shore." It was the same place where Fred had gone while growing up. She deserved it, and so did he. This job could wait. His team had been chasing the *Hermit*, a fifty-four-foot wooden sailboat running hashish, all over the world. The *Hermit* was a prestigious yacht-race contender, and due to its wood construction, it had avoided the Coast Guard's radar detection. After sailing from England then picking up drugs from Berber tribesmen in Morocco, the boat had finally landed near New York where the smugglers had transferred over a ton of hashish onto waiting speedboats, then into trucks, and on to a warehouse in Mystic, Connecticut. But with good information from a reliable stool, actually Jack the factory owner, the drugs had been seized in a well-coordinated bust. That should have been the end of the case, but four of the smugglers escaped on the *Hermit*. Now they could be anywhere on the ocean, and it was as good a time as any for Fred to head home to his family.

━━

THREE DAYS LATER, he called his house from an airport payphone. "Tell Suzie I'm on my way home! I'll be there as soon as possible." He imagined Ginger smiling on the other end of the line.

While Ginger helped a wriggling Suzie get ready for the shore, Fred darted out of the airport and into his government car. But on the way home he got a call on the two-way radio.

It was the DEA communication center, who immediately patched him directly to a Navy fighter pilot. Over loud mechanical sounds and a rhythmic engine hum, the voice of the fighter pilot crackled through. "I've spotted your elusive sailboat off the coast of Bermuda."

The pilot gave his location, and Fred mentally pictured the wooden sailboat with its billowing sails cutting through the waves on its way to Bermuda but still many miles away.

"Are you sure it's the *Hermit*?" Fred asked.

"Yep. But I'll check again…"

"No! Don't do that. You'll spook them. Move on and fly back over in a while."

"Too late. I just passed over the boat at fifty feet off the water, and it says *Hermit* on the stern. I'm circling again over the occupants right now." His voice was livid with excitement.

Fred's heart raced. The Navy pilot was inexperienced in the techniques of surveillance and had unknowingly warned the smugglers that they were being followed. Still, the operation had reached its crescendo. Hopefully all the weeks of stakeouts and undercover work were about to pay off.

⊏⊐

WHEN HE ARRIVED home and opened the door, there stood Suzie in a pink swimsuit wearing a plastic floating ring around her waist. "Daddy!" she squealed, jumping up and down.

Fred knelt down next to his baby girl, and his voice cracked. "I'm sorry, Suzie. I only came home to get fresh clothes. We'll go to the shore as soon as I come back though." He rose to his feet and looked at Ginger whose face had fallen into despair. "I have to fly right back to Bermuda tomorrow morning." He rested a hand on his wife's shoulder.

Suzie's face crumpled, and she strained bravely to hold back the tears that were running down her face. Ginger clapped a hand over her mouth, turned away, and burst into sobs.

The next morning Fred flew to Bermuda consumed with sadness and guilt over Ginger and Suzie. He couldn't just tell the bosses it wasn't a good day for him to go to Bermuda. The commitment to this job was unconditional, but something had to change. Whenever he thought things might slow down, they only sped up. The sickness he felt in his heart stretched to his gut. He couldn't remember ever feeling so low. He was trapped between a demanding job and a family he loved, and how did it ever get to this point? He had an inkling of a plan in the back of his mind, but then the plane touched down on the tropical island, and he spun into investigative mode.

When Fred arrived in Bermuda, the *Hermit* was docked in Hamilton Harbor. He met with Inspector Monez, a Bermuda police lieutenant. They stepped outside into the sunshine, and Monez ushered him into the "clubhouse" near the police department. It was a perfectly square and windowless one-story building painted light pink. Inside the room were rickety tables, and each one bore several black burn scars where cigarettes had lain. Around the tables sat policemen talking, joking, and drinking anything from bottles of beer to whiskey (but usually beer). There were no pictures to adorn the walls, and the only bathroom was dank with a cracked sink and rusty toilet. Although not surprisingly there were four refrigerators along one wall in the main room. The entire setup was noticeably plain, with the exception of an ornately carved wooden bar decked out with a brass rail and fittings. It looked as though it had been plucked from a 19th century New York restaurant and now sat awkwardly among the inferior furnishings.

Monez motioned for Fred to sit down, and the police commissioner, Leroy "Nobby" Clark, fumbled through some cardboard boxes before producing a couple bottles of Killian's Irish Red beer.

"It's happy hour!" he beckoned, lifting the bottle in a cheer before popping the top off. "Every day is happy hour when you work with us in Bermuda." He lightly slapped Fred on the back.

And it was. Every morning for the next five days, they started out with a liquid breakfast and "worked" until early afternoon when everyone had reached the point of no longer being an asset to their job. Most of the 'work' involved watching *The Hermit* for suspicious activity from the comfort of a beach chair. While whiling away the mornings at the clubhouse, Fred learned a great deal about Monez and Nobby. They were both committed police officers but were surely from different molds. Monez was as straight as any arrow had ever been, while Clark lived by his own set of rules—not a particularly bad set of rules, but his own, nonetheless. And one thing was certain. As with most of the police officers he met, Monez and Clark both liked to drink. Again, there was a difference: Monez drank his share, but Nobby drank every share he could get his hands on.

FRED'S previous inkling of a plan unfolded with a flourish. He arranged to have Ginger flown to Bermuda while Suzie stayed with

Ginger's mom for three days. Fred eventually regretted having Monez accompany him to the airport to get her. When Ginger arrived, Monez greeted her island style, warmly and with open arms. "Welcome! Your husband has been working all morning and is probably ready for his afternoon rest." He pointed to Fred who was standing on wobbly beer-infused legs. In the car she sat between the two of them and could hardly get a breath of air that wasn't saturated with the smell of alcohol. She whispered in Fred's ear, "This is what you call hard work?"

"It's not always like this. It's just a little Bermuda custom," he assured her.

After three days, a DEA agent who was coming to Bermuda accompanied Suzie on a flight so the family could have some time together. "Is that safe?" Ginger questioned. "Make sure she's safe. Remember, I was in labor four months with that child," she said with typical Giner humor. "She's pretty special to me."

During this time, the Bermuda police continued watching the *Hermit* every hour of every day as the crew cleaned it, outfitted it with supplies, checked the sails and other equipment, and visited local bars and restaurants rather routinely. Then they returned every night to sleep on the vessel. They didn't seem to have a care in the world and were oblivious to the police attention. Fred occasionally helped with surveillance but spent most mornings at the clubhouse and most afternoons on the beach with Ginger and Suzie. As it turned out, the leisurely pace helped soothe Suzie's broken heart. Fred still reeled at the pain he'd inflicted on his little girl when he'd ruined her dream weekend. The unexpected trip to Bermuda helped, but didn't eliminate his feelings of guilt.

A few days after Fred, Ginger, and Suzie had been enjoying the pink Bermuda sand, Monez confided that he and his fellow officers would be spending the day searching the sailboat.

Just as the sun rose to high noon, the group of lawmen walked down the dock toward the *Hermit* and its crew.

The boat's skipper was an American, Captain Dan Caton. "What do you want?" he asked upon seeing Monez approaching.

Monez identified himself, surveyed Caton and the vessel with confidence then simply said, "We'll be searching the boat now." He brushed past Caton, and upon receiving no resistance, the rest of the police officers followed. With Caton looking on unconcerned, they searched every crevice and container on the *Hermit*. Five hours later, Monez called a halt to the search, and they filed off the boat and back to the clubhouse. The search had turned up nothing. Not even a single marijuana cigarette. It had failed.

Disappointed, Fred asked Monez what he planned to do now.

"Just watch," Monez wagged a finger at him then turned and went back to the boat where he advised Caton that he and the crew were being arrested for Piracy on the High Seas. And then he took them all into custody.

Fred didn't interfere but was curious about this action. After all, they hadn't found any contraband, and they certainly did not have the authority to arrest the crew for a crime in the United States. Fred didn't have that ability either and would have needed a provisional arrest authority from a U.S. court. Finally he asked Monez about it. Monez smiled for the first time since they'd met and said with self-satisfaction, "I don't even know what the piracy would be, but I'd guess the Queen would approve. So we will find *something* these pirates have done." They both laughed vigorously. Piracy was an old Bermuda law that had been on the books for ages.

"Piracy? Not one of them has a wooden leg or one of those Jolly Roger flags," Fred joked, pleased at his own wit. His engaging humor had made him immediately popular with the local law enforcement officers who regularly sought him out to join them in whatever they were doing. Usually drinking.

The four crew members of the *Hermit* found themselves under arrest and in a decrepit Bermuda jail cell. The floor was laden with several centimeters of dirty water, which was partially to blame for the rampant rat infestation. Some of the prisoners survived by wrapping up in their thin, damp blanket to protect themselves from being bitten by rodents and tropical bugs.

The crew of the *Hermit* remained in the filthy jail cell with little food for five more days before Monez came to talk with them. "You pirates must know that here in Bermuda we investigate a crime as fast as the snail crawls. You might be in your cells for a very long time, unless you want to talk to the American Special Agent to see what he could do for you."

At first they refused and demanded lawyers. A couple of days later, they changed their minds and each of the smugglers signed extradition papers allowing them to be sent back to the United States for prosecution and to be used as informants. Before being sent back, Fred was assigned to interview one of the women crew members.

"My official title was 'cook,' but I think they just brought me along because I'm good at oral sex," she said, a bit seductively.

"That's fine," Fred replied, "but we won't put that in the report."

Later Suzie again got to go to the beach with her dad and splash in the waves, but their break would be short-lived. A hodgepodge of open cases awaited Fred and his group in New York.

AFTER REFLECTING BACK on his months away from the family, working on the *Hermit* case and other time-consuming projects, Fred agreed with Ginger. Things had started getting out of control again with too much work. "Give me a few more weeks to wrap things up, and I promise to make our family a priority."

CHAPTER
TWENTY-NINE

NEW JERSEY
Early 1978

FRED ARRIVED home not only a day earlier than he'd expected but well before dinner. Ginger had kidded him about bringing some of the Florida sunshine with him when he returned. However, the only remnant he brought from the southern state was a case of cynicism brought on by something he'd read in a newspaper on the plane. It was another "marijuana is a harmless drug" article, and it had him rankled. He wouldn't let the negative attitude affect his family though, so he swallowed the irritation. He'd release it later on in private. It was a mental trick he'd learned during his years as a basketball player when he'd had to set aside worry about his dad possibly losing the family home due to financial problems. He'd block it out, focus on the game, and deal with the problem later.

He stood on the front step forcing the negative thoughts aside until his mouth finally gyrated itself into a genuine grin. Then he opened the door.

"Fred!" Ginger emerged from the kitchen wearing an apron and rushed to greet him. He hugged and kissed her and the kids in turn and while bouncing Dave on one knee, he carefully extracted himself from the vice grip Suzie had around his neck. He pulled several seashells from his pocket, which he held tightly in his palm before revealing them in a flash, as though he'd just performed magic. Suzie squealed, and little Dave quickly snatched one and tried to put it in his mouth, which brought a round of protests from Suzie who cried, "They're *mine!*"

While he reunited with the kids, Ginger unpacked his suitcase, putting dirty clothes in one pile and holding up a still-folded shirt to see if it needed washing or ironing. "You know, Fred, the seashells are a much better choice than your previous gifts," Ginger said, referring to the shelf full of shot glasses he'd brought his young daughter on prior trips.

"They're colorful and only a buck each. I can always find them in the airport gift shop," he'd explained every time Ginger rolled her eyes at the small ceramic vessels for intoxication. Now she was eyeing him somewhat uneasily, and then clapped her hands and announced they were going to "let daddy take a shower while we get dinner ready." She could sense when he had something on his mind.

Minutes later he was breathing in the thick steam and letting hot jets of water pound on the tension in his neck and back. The stress lessened, and after a rare family dinner together, they got the kids into the tub—he gave in to Suzie's pleas for lots of bubbles—and finally into bed. After Suzie asked for water and two more stories, he and Ginger relaxed on the couch.

"So," she began carefully, "something bothering you?"

Fred hemmed and hawed. He didn't like burdening her with work problems. "You know, we risk our lives every day trying to do what's right. In the last week I've heard at least three people excuse their behavior by saying pot is a harmless drug. I've even read it in a newspaper! It may seem that way on the surface. I suppose when you compare marijuana's physical effects on the body to heroin or cocaine, it's milder." He shook his head and took a long drink. He couldn't help but notice what a good listener Ginger was. She could block out the whole world and focus only on her family, which was a trait he tried to emulate.

"Go ahead. I know there's more."

"Well, it's *such* one-dimensional thinking. The issue of marijuana goes much deeper. We see so many people start with 'just' smoking pot before moving on to harder drugs. And the money people spend on pot and other drugs," he spread his arms wide, "it would make you sick. Ginger, we see these druggie parents neglect the needs of their children, and I'm talking no food in the house because every extra penny goes for drugs. And it's not just the people buying it. There's so much money to be made in the marijuana business, and with illegal money you're sure to find excessive violence and other crimes right on its tail."

"Not to mention the cops who get shot and...other people, like Special Agents." She pulled him closer.

Fred nodded. There was no denying that it was an underlying worry every day for him. "Most people don't know that in many countries where the pot is grown, they make little kids work all day long picking and bundling the stuff." His thoughts went right to Suzie and Dave. He wished every child had a safe home. "Anyway, the next time someone tells me pot is harmless, I'd like them to be the one to go knock on the door in Florida. And when the mother of the two McAdams sisters answers, tell her we found your girls at the bottom of a sinkhole shot in the head. Oh, but by the way, marijuana is harmless."

Fred fought back the sadness, and Ginger squeezed his hand, allowing him to process the thoughts without interrupting. It was something he needed at the moment.

CHAPTER
THIRTY

TEXAS
Mid-1970s

CHARLES "MUSCLES" Foster, in spite of his odious appearance was, in a sense, a starry-eyed romantic. The need for a woman's company was as vital to him as oxygen. And he didn't want just any woman. She had to adore him, and in return he would treasure her to the extent he was capable. So it was that after each of his three failed marriages, he took off for weeks at a time due to despair. He just up and disappeared, eventually showing up at the doorstep of a friend or relative halfway across the country. His third marriage had produced two boys, and when this wife left in 1965 with his sons in tow, Muscles turned to Poppa Rex Cauble for help. He reportedly got $9,000 from Rex to lure back his bride, and while she happily took the money, she did not take Muscles back. This threw him into an emotional nosedive.

It was at this point that Muscles decided his only option was suicide. One day he was discovered convulsing, and when that problem was under control Muscles was secured in a straitjacket and taken to a mental health facility. Many of his friends didn't realize where he was, assuming he'd taken off after another broken heart. But upon his return, Muscles appeared to have regressed. He took to drinking heavily, and his best friend, Willis Judge Butler, was concerned when Muscles fretted about losing all his memory.

Over the years Muscles would receive at least thirty-one electroshock treatments, which resulted in insomnia and difficulty remembering names. Muscles worried. His father had suffered from depression and died in a state hospital. Some close to him chalked it up to Muscles being a compulsive exaggerator, and felt his actions and responses were inconsistent. Perhaps at first he experienced those symptoms, but his ability to orchestrate the massive marijuana operation told a different story. As the drug ring flourished, so did Muscles's confidence in proclaiming himself the lord of the drug ring. He used it when it benefited him, such as positioning himself as the boss to any of the men in the drug operation he considered to be an underling.

Muscles could hardly go bragging to beautiful women in bars that he was a drug kingpin, so he came up with another strategy. He flashed rolls of $100 bills, bragging about all the ranches he was in charge of. He was making so much money, he took to offering women Cadillacs in exchange for sexual favors that he hoped would segue into a solid relationship once the woman realized what he had not only in bed but financially. What woman wouldn't want to attach her star to someone not only sexually gifted but who could also provide the finer things in life?

On one particular night, Muscles sought out a lovely woman at the bar and bought her a drink. He made friendly conversation, something that came easily to him, but she wasn't interested and in fact was repulsed by his homely face.

"Thanks for the drink, but I'm meeting friends shortly," she politely lied.

"Drinks? Did you think I was buying you drinks in hopes we'd…" he trailed off with a chuckle. "Look, you're a beautiful girl, and I have a lot to offer you. More than any other common laborer in this tacky bar could ever give you. Take a look outside. I got a beautiful Cadillac sitting out there, and she's all yours. All I want is one night with you."

Of course, he didn't want just one night. He hoped that after one night the girl would come to her senses and agree to be his wife, but that never happened. Month after month it didn't happen. Most women continued to reject the odd little cowboy. But some did exchange sex for lavish gifts. He repeatedly gave away a Cadillac to almost any woman who would take him up on the offer, but they too all left after hours or days, and he went through the following weeks brokenhearted and lost. Perhaps it was partly due to his passion for promising more than he could deliver. He did the same with his partners in the drug trade. He never paid them nearly what he promised he would, always followed by the excuse of not netting the amount they should have, or having gotten ripped off somewhere in the process. So it was with the many women. He didn't quite measure up to be what he'd promised.

So many women turned down the offer of the Cadillac that Muscles developed a new strategy. "You don't have to sleep with me," he explained to a woman who had already walked away from him and refused further offers of alcohol. "You can satisfy me any way you want, like with your mouth, and I'll give you a motorcycle instead." Again his offer fell flat, and Muscles woke up the next day with nothing but a hangover to show for it.

"Buy a hooker," his friends begged him. "You could have a year of hookers for what one of those Cadillacs costs you." But he didn't want a hooker. He wanted a wife who loved him like no other.

But riding on Poppa Rex's coattails brought him the air of respectability he so craved. On New Year's Eve, as 1977 crept into 1978, Muscles partied away in Las Vegas with Rex by his side. However, Muscles in his worn and faded cowboy-casual t-shirt and jeans paled next to the dapper Rex.

On April 8, 1978, they returned to Vegas so Rex could play in the World Series of Poker. Not being much of a poker player, Rex quickly lost the $10,000 entry fee, but somehow returned to Texas with lots of cash he needed to deposit in the Dallas International Bank. He'd supposedly won $260,000 in other gambling ventures. The chairman of the bank refused to deposit the money and suggested that Rex put it in one of his own banks. In reality, this was not too much of a problem since Cauble Enterprises was on a list of businesses that were exempt from having to have cash deposits over $10,000 reported to the IRS. By the end of 1978, Cauble Enterprises had almost $700,000 in cash deposited in its special account. But that would not immediately raise a red flag.

CHAPTER
THIRTY-ONE

TEXAS
February 2, 1978

THE SPECIAL AGENTS in Texas had been gathering vital information regarding a potential widespread drug-smuggling ring for many months. It had started in Georgia where agents were running surveillance on Raymond Hawkins. The airplane that arrived to pick him up had "Cauble Enterprises" emblazoned on the side. That had been the first possible link to Rex. Then agents gathered phone and credit card records. They even collected Rex's garbage and found notes with the names "Muscles" and "Katko." Then there were the suspicious banking transactions with extremely large cash deposits. The dragnet had widened and the comings and goings around the Cauble properties were being tracked. The feds wondered how Cauble could be nonchalant about having business dealings with convicted drug dealers Hawkins and Gerdes.

Two Texas law enforcement officers sat just down the lane intently watching the Cauble ranch, jotting notes on vehicles coming and going. They'd been informed about Muscles and drugs potentially being run through the Cauble properties. A car left the ranch and pulled up alongside the agents' vehicle. It was former Texas state narcotics officer Bill Clifton, a pleasant well-mannered man, tall and muscular with cowboy good looks. He stopped to chat with the two agents who were undercover observing the ranch in their unmarked car.

Years ago, The Old Man had become so impressed with the way Clifton had handled a local situation that he'd offered the officer a job as general manager at his Miley Trailer firm for two times the pay he was getting as a Texas lawman. Clifton, being a young man in need of money, was enticed by a job that would pay so well. He accepted the offer and resigned as a state narcotics officer.

It was just a lighthearted and casual conversation between Clifton and the two Texas agents as they sat talking in the afternoon sun. A few minutes later, another vehicle approached them from the opposite direction, slowing to a near crawl as it approached the agents' state car. The occupants wore cowboy hats tipped low on their heads, and though dark sunglasses concealed their eyes it was obvious they were staring intensely at the former narcotics officer. Just when it appeared they were about to stop, the car sped over the crest of a hill. It was unsettling.

———

THREE DAYS later Clifton sat in his vehicle waiting for a red light to change when an old Chevy rolled up alongside him. When the light turned green, a powerful shotgun blast blew the side of Clifton's face away and knocked his bottom jaw off. Later, a police officer who had responded to the call retrieved Clifton's jaw from the street. He placed it on the dashboard of the bloody car so it could be used as evidence when the detectives arrived at the crime site.

Although Clifton lost his jaw, most of his teeth, his lips, and parts of his nose and tongue, he survived. The sharp-looking young man would be forever disfigured. For the next year he was in and out of hospitals for numerous reconstructive surgeries, with Cauble paying not only his medical expenses but his salary as well.

The shooting was never solved. Clifton thought he knew who it was—someone he'd had to fire at one of Cauble's operations. Even though Clifton apparently had no connection to the smugglers, agents theorized that it was possibly a violent message being sent by the drug runners: If anyone in Rex's realm cooperated or talked to law enforcement, they would pay a heavy price. The surveillance on the Cauble ranches continued. It would only be one short month before two men would be arrested by the Orange County Texas Sheriff's Department for smuggling 1,000 pounds of marijuana on the shrimper *Bayou Blues*. The two arrested told authorities that Muscles was involved in the operation, adding more reason to keep focus on the Cauble ranches. The Special Agents in New York would soon discover that their Texas comrades had already started the ball rolling.

CHAPTER
THIRTY-TWO

TEXAS/COLOMBIA
November 1978

REX CAUBLE not only liked surrounding himself with horse-loving cowboy types but also anyone with notoriety. Rex found someone who checked both boxes when he hired Les Fuller, who had supposedly been a Marlboro Man model. Marlboro cigarettes were a popular brand, and equally as popular were their commercials on TV featuring the Marlboro Man, a handsome and rugged guy dressed in western wear, cowboy hat, and with a cigarette hanging out of his mouth. Thus, those close to Les sometimes referred to him as the Marlboro Man.

Because of this cowboy image, Rex hired Les to work at his Cutter Bill's Western World where Les eventually became the president. However, he was not a good one, and the stores were hemorrhaging money under his watch. On top of that, Les had a temper just as fiery as his boss. He didn't take kindly to getting his butt chewed by Rex in the same way someone would scold a small child. The shrewd money-making Rex couldn't tolerate the personality clash and poor management skills and had to fire him. At almost fifty years old, Les felt washed up, and spiraled into depression.

It so happened that losing his job at Cutter Bill's Western World was not the worst thing that could have happened to Les Fuller, though it seemed to him at the time that it was. His conversations with Willis Judge Butler was what really sent him spinning on a downward track. Willis needed someone to go to South America with him (they'd get rich) on November 8, and Les had no other business prospects on the horizon. *Get rich* kept pounding through his brain.

Right from the start, Les's ability to attract bad luck carried him straight through to this next venture. They would be travelling on a newly purchased boat, the *Agnes Pauline* or *Aggie* as they'd nicknamed her. Les inserted himself into the operation from the start and had what would turn out to be justified concerns about the radar and other equipment being installed. He was having problems with the captain, Charles Busby, over outfitting the shrimper. Fuller went to his friend Jim Brooks and asked him to sink the *Aggie*, but Brooks wouldn't do it. It became such a point of contention that Fuller offered Willis $5,000 to kill Busby and his girlfriend. Willis refused, and in addition put a stop to the plan to sink the boat. With some smooth talking, he assured Les that the shrimper was safe, and they packed for the trip. However, Busby was fired as captain.

Les brought his girlfriend Gloria Davis, who was eager to write about the adventure in the daily diary she kept. Accompanying Willis was his girlfriend, Holly Mosel. Fortunately, there was a new captain with them. Gloria noted in her journal that the other two men barely knew how to adjust the wires and rods of the masts on the seventy-three-foot *Agnes Pauline*. This turned out to be unfortunate, since two days into the trip, the captain was so strung out on heroin that he couldn't leave his room. Gloria wrote that, "Doors were banging open and shut, the portable radio and miscellaneous items slid off the table, and the biggie happened. The refrigerator door flew open and spit out 5 gallons of milk, a bottle of salad dressing, two bottles of orange juice, a jar of strawberry jam, and a can of 7-Up."

The boat started leaking heavily, and everyone onboard used buckets to bail out the flow of water. On top of that, Les was fighting intense pain from frequent kidney-stone attacks. The women were seasick. Since the new captain was unable to navigate the boat, Les took over. Then, as if that weren't enough misfortune, the shrimper lost radio contact and Les had to use an old-world sailing sextant to guide them to Colombia.

Les and Willis learned to work the rigging enough to stop the *Aggie* from going into a fatal rollover. Through strobe-light flashes of lightning, she chugged toward her destination. The wind was relentless. Water had been streaming in before Galveston was even out of sight, which should have been their warning to ditch the whole deal. But there was a fortune in marijuana waiting for them in Colombia, and the thought of a big payout kept them going.

Although the shrimper had been fitted with expensive equipment including sonar and radar, all of it—even the pumps—eventually quit working at various points throughout the voyage. After nine days of relentless problems, the *Aggie* finally anchored off the Colombian shore during a fierce storm. Rain shot down like bullets, the ocean swells battered the sides of the swaying shrimper, and it was in the middle of the night when someone realized the anchor line had broken. They were drifting back into sharp rocks in forty-five-mile-an-hour winds. They had no choice but to steer straight into the storm.

That turned out to be the least of their problems. Twenty-four hours went by with no word from their Colombian connection, Big Pete. Then it was forty-eight hours and then seventy-two hours. To avoid drawing suspicion, they trawled up and down the coast wondering what to do, until they finally got word that the delivery would be delayed for three more days. Gloria wrote, "If we didn't have bad luck, we wouldn't have any."

At midnight of the third day, Big Pete sent several small boats out to the *Aggie*, and there was a frenzy to throw the bales of marijuana aboard. Twenty-two tons in all. They didn't finish until dawn, exhausted.

The trip back to Texas went smoother, and that seemed like a good omen. Below deck sat twenty-two tons of high-grade "red bud" marijuana packed in ice. They took turns sitting atop the bales of pot while posing with automatic weapons and staring threateningly into the camera. Les was exhilarated and already wanting to make another run. After a streak of hard times in his life, he finally felt like a success.

On November 29, 1978, three weeks after they first left Galveston, the coast of Texas was once again in sight. Rather than using one of the secluded docks, they sailed right into the bustling crowd at the Quality Seafood Docks in Port Arthur. Once the *Aggie* came to rest, they realized that the smell of pot was overwhelming. It didn't matter. The feds had been watching the *Aggie* for months and knew that she was headed to port with a cargo full of drugs. The minute a crew showed up to help unload the boat, agents swarmed the leaky shrimper.

Twelve people were arrested right at the dock, and the cargo full of marijuana, which carried a street value between twelve and twenty-four million, was hailed as a major drug bust. But right away, Special Agents were itching to find "The Big One"—the one who was financially backing the whole operation. At first, they believed it was Les Fuller, but once he cracked and started spilling names, the feds aimed their sights on Muscles, Carlos Gerdes, Raymond Hawkins, and John Ruppel, who owned the *Aggie*. For now, Rex Cauble's name officially stayed out of the limelight, but only because government agents had begun a grand jury investigation and were still collecting information on his banks and businesses. The Old Man was definitely in the spotlight.

The *Aggie* bust was big, and by early May of 1979, a federal grand jury had wrapped up a six-month investigation into the alleged narcotics trafficking operation nicknamed the "Cowboy Mafia" by a Dallas newspaper. They returned indictments against twenty-four people, and evidence showed at a minimum, 176,000 pounds of marijuana being smuggled over an eighteen-month period, though it was suspected there was more.

CHAPTER
THIRTY-THREE

TEXAS
Early December 1978

FRED AND HATCH found themselves flying to the Lone Star state. Denton, Texas, home of the self-made millionaire Rex Cauble, boasted a population of 30,000 when Rex was building his fortune in the 1960s. The fierce independence of a pioneering spirit swept through the town the way tumbleweeds had done so many decades before. The cowboy life with trusty steeds, barbecue cookouts, open ranges, and rodeos was a testament to the untamed nature surrounding Denton. The town was named after John B. Denton, a pioneer preacher and lawyer who was killed during an Indian fight in 1841. It became a settlement in 1843, and two colleges came along in 1890. There was an unmistakable atmosphere of Texas hospitality where people knew their neighbors and helped each other out. Rustic saloons still thrived in Denton's business district, where one could imagine the wooden swinging doors of years gone by that let out the sound of ragtime music and raucous laughter. Cowboys could still gather here after a hard day's work, slap the dust off their blue jeans, and down shots of strong whiskey.

It was in this bustling town with its unparalleled work ethic that Texas DEA agents had collected a mountain of evidence. In an investigation of this magnitude, however, the amount that needed to be collected was nearly endless. Fred paged through folders brimming with information on The Old Man and Muscles: bank statements showing large cash deposits, business records, surveillance, and code-fendants giving statements against the two. A picture was coming into focus of an expansive, lucrative, and illegal drug organization. It was then that they fully understood both the extent of the marijuana opera-tion that spread throughout the country, with the cocaine business mostly limited to the east coast.

Fred unpacked his suitcase in the dim light of yet another strange hotel room. He pushed some shirts aside looking for the note he knew Suzie had hidden somewhere in his belongings. It was a new tradition she'd started since learning to write, and the first thing Fred did when unpacking was to read the note. He found a wrinkled envelope with large childlike writing on the outside that said "Dad." He opened it, imagining the smile on Suzie's face when she'd snuck in his room the previous night to hide her letter.

I Love you come home soon!

He set the note on the nightstand next to his bed and then went to the window and peered outside to scan the parking lot. DEA agents were trained to minimize risk, and in this case it had meant even keeping the location of their Denton hotel room confidential. An agent could be wacked the same as a stool, especially in very big drug cases. The Old Man was well-liked by the local law enforcement groups, having endeared himself through social interactions. He put on cook-outs and donated money to the state police. He was even a member of the Special Texas Rangers, and the Texas Rangers considered Rex a close friend. He'd contributed money to their organization and helped with other initiatives throughout the years.

Realistically, Fred and his team had to acknowledge the possibility that any particular lawman could be beholden to The Old Man, be on the take, or be susceptible to a potential bribe.

There was something else concerning. The Texas DEA Special Agents seemed solidly trustworthy. They'd even alerted Fred to a couple of possible leaks. Fred, Hatch, and Redden discussed it. Could the DEA agents have inadvertently revealed info while drinking with a friend from another law enforcement agency, which wasn't infrequent? Possibly. All of a sudden, there were various men who operated within the many law enforcement groups who seemed to have information about the case that they shouldn't be privy to.

One of the Texas Special Agents pulled Fred aside into a conference room and closed the door. "I'm starting to be concerned. Just watch yourself. When you guys from New York are down here, we suddenly seem to have a whole lot more outsiders in our office." By outsiders he meant the whole array of local and state lawmen.

Later that day, Fred was again in the Texas office when he went into an empty room to get some coffee. A local police officer came up next to him, so Fred held out his hand and said, "I'm Fred Boff." The officer didn't extend a hand. Fred knew it was always a bad sign when someone refused a handshake. The conversation quickly went awry. The officer folded his arms across his chest stormily and said, "You're the big shot from New York." Fred replied he was, and the officer continued. "Rex Cauble is a fine and upstanding citizen. I think you know what I mean."

Fred shrugged.

"Just remember that a lot of people come down here from up north. Sometimes they never go back home," the man added.

Fred didn't break eye contact. He wouldn't put himself in the subordinate position of responding to this man's veiled threat, and instead took control by steering the conversation back to where he wanted it. "What the hell does that mean?"

"Nothing. I'm just trying to tell you that people disappear. It's a big state."

"That sounds like a threat to me."

"No, no, no. I wouldn't threaten you. You're a fed." The officer's face took on a smug look, but Fred didn't budge. He was nearly immune to such intimidation and had seen better attempts at this from petty street thugs. Still, this veiled threat could not be ignored. If the statement had been made in front of a group, Fred could have possibly taken it differently. But this officer had made a point of cornering Fred alone. There was a real possibility that any particular law enforcement group could be in bed with Rex Cauble, due to the wide net of endowment he'd cast across this region of Texas.

Fred talked to his Assistant Special Agent in Charge who was concerned, so he then directed Fred to speak with the Special Agent in Charge.

Fred did, and the SAIC was equally concerned. "This is between you and me, Fred. Just act normal, make your travel arrangements, and get a rental car. Get a hotel. But I'm going to arrange to give you cash to pay for everything. I want you to travel with cash only so you won't be so easy to track."

It was a good plan. Fred could purchase an airline ticket, hotel, and rental car with cash only. No credit card was required.

"Don't tell anyone where you're staying. Once you leave a hotel, don't go back. Pick a different hotel the next night. And you need to take this situation to headquarters." It was not a suggestion that was ever given lightly, and soon Fred was on a plane to Washington, D.C., to meet with a headquarters' Division Chief.

———

"REX CAUBLE?" the Chief said upon hearing a brief summary of the Texas case. His eyes brightened, and he sat up straighter. "Now there's a name I haven't heard in some years! Don't you think you're being paranoid?" There was an obvious remnant of a Texas drawl in his speech. "Let me tell you about Rex Cauble. From the time I was this high," he said holding a hand about three feet off the ground, "I have admired what Rex Cauble has done for the state of Texas and this country. He's a generous man with dedication to upholding the law, especially regarding drug use. Ol' Rex was a big part of my inspiration to enter law enforcement. If you go after Rex Cauble, you better get him."

Some of the details Fred expected to hear from the Chief never came forth. He never said he'd look into it or would keep Fred advised. He didn't ask if Fred had received any suspicious phone calls or if anyone was following him. While neither of those had yet occurred, there seemed to be absolutely no concern, and Fred chalked it up to the Division Chief being misguided due to the way he idolized Rex. Fred didn't feel the Chief was being dishonest, but the lack of concern was frustrating.

WHILE FRED WORKED IN TEXAS, he continued to pay for everything in cash so that there was no record of where he was staying. (Still, he slept with his gun on the nightstand.)

The case moved forward, and he and Hatch would be interviewing Muscles who had voluntarily agreed to speak with the Special Agents.

Ginger had once asked him why criminals who were clearly guilty would agree to talk with him. "You're trying to put them in *prison*. Shouldn't they try to avoid you?"

"Deceit, honey. Deceit," he'd answered. "These guys think they're slick enough to feed me false information and steer me away from what they've done. They're convinced they can make me think I've got the wrong guy and send me down other paths. But you know, Ginger, deceit goes both ways. I know how to make these scumbags think I'm on their side, and when they relax just enough to open up and make themselves vulnerable, I get the ammunition I need to use against them."

"And that's how you win the game for the good guys? Deceit?"

"Yep. We fight fire with fire. And we dangle the carrot. We let them know their future is in our hands, and we tell them how much time they're looking at and that we might be able to help them if they cooperate. We make them think we're the only ones on the planet who can help them." Fred was exceptionally skilled in doing this even with hardened criminals.

LATER THAT DAY, Fred and Hatch were assigned an interview room at an attorney's office where they got their first look at Muscles. Both agents had experienced their share of being surprised by a suspect who didn't fit into one of the stereotypes of the "typical drug dealer"—the big tough Mafioso type, the scrawny long-haired street dealer, the white-collar cocaine-dealing businessman, and so on. Muscles's appearance, however, made them both do a double take. Scrawny with ears sprouting from his head like satellite dishes and an odd-looking home-style haircut, he didn't have the same high-roller appearance of the other Texas suspects they'd investigated.

During introductions, Muscles shook hands with the agents. His grip was unusually soft and limp. Fred and Hatch started with some casual conversation and observations to ease into the interview, but Muscles made no response other than some involuntary body spasms. His face revealed no effect.

"You've been informed about the case we're looking into, so let's proceed," Hatch began, straightening his notepad on the table. "Can you tell us when you first became involved with Rex Cauble?"

Muscles sat slumped in his chair. His mouth twitched. After a long pause, he drew in a deep breath and said somewhat incoherently, "I was eight...years...old when my, my, uh, my mom..." His voice trailed off. Hatch and Fred waited, puzzled by where the sentence was headed. "...she bought me a pony. A black and...black-and-white... pony."

Hatch started to restate the question, "How old were you when you first—"

"He was a...a...a gentle little guy. That p-pony." Muscles looked not at, but through, the agents with a faraway stare as though he barely realized they were in the same room.

Fred and Hatch exchanged a what-the-hell look. Fred gave it a try, something more direct that might grab Muscles's attention. "Did you ever see drugs—marijuana—on Rex Cauble's ranch?"

Muscles sat for nearly two minutes, but the agents were ready to wait him out. Too much silence became uncomfortable, and subjects would usually respond by filling the void with words. Drool dribbled from the corner of Muscles's mouth, but still they waited, and he finally spoke. "When I got ol...older, my f-first car was...red. Red. It didn't go so...so fast."

"Look, Muscles (one of the only coherent statements he'd made was during introductions when he'd told them to "call me Muscles"), let's focus on a few of our questions," Hatch said with the commanding yet encouraging voice he possessed that made him invaluable during interviews. "Did you ever hear of Rex Cauble's plane being used to fly drugs into or out of his ranch?"

Muscles contorted his body, and he went deeper into a distant stare. His eyes didn't blink the whole time. "I like the lake when the weather is warm," he murmured.

The agents continued asking questions, reasoning that if this was an act, he might slip up or get tired of the ruse. The interview continued down the bizarre path for a long time until Fred called a stop to it. They thanked Muscles for coming and didn't demonstrate any body language that would reveal their frustration lest that was Muscles's whole intent.

"Is this guy screwed up?" Hatch asked after Muscles left.

"The guy is either on drugs, crazy, or just putting on the nutty show for us. We'll simply have to nail him with the evidence that's piling up." Fred's gut feeling was that Muscles was pulling a "Vincent."

MUSCLES'S ATTORNEY contacted Fred and Hatch a few weeks later and offered to let them interview his client, this time with the attorney present. During the second interview Muscles appeared much more lucid, and he answered at least some of the questions. He told when he met Rex and what jobs he performed on the ranches. He willingly answered questions about the many women in bars whom he'd gifted with Cadillacs—there had been at least a dozen. He seemed pleased that he'd been able to "catch" so many hot dates this way.

"Muscles, I wish I'd had that technique in college," Fred joked. This friendly banter that came so easily to Fred was designed to lull the person being interviewed into becoming comfortable enough to open up. Muscles never did reach a level of trust, and remained guarded.

It was obvious in reading between the lines that Muscles wanted a relationship. He'd had three failed marriages, and each failure had left him feeling miserable and without hope. He even tried working his way into the lives of the Special Agents. Muscles first built himself up as the head of all of Rex's ranches and emphasized the enormous business finesse that required. He added in his recent success with some rather desirable women, and then when he felt he'd portrayed himself as quite the big shot, he said, "Maybe when this is all over, we can get together and talk. You know, just shoot the breeze."

Fred and Hatch nodded noncommittally. They had no intention of ever being Muscles's buddies.

The one area of questioning that caused Muscles to jump like a radioactive Geiger counter was anything related to The Old Man's involvement with drugs.

"You got him wrong!" Muscles shouted, leaning forward and suddenly full of spirit. "Rex is a good person. A real good person." His mouth twisted, and he scooted around in his chair. "He's been the best poppa anyone could ask for!"

Fred leaned forward looking Muscles right in the eye. "Just to let you know, we'll be checking out The Old Man and you every which way we can think of."

The way Muscles fluctuated from sane to disjointed caused Fred to wonder if they were dealing with another Vincent "The Chin" Gigante, the infamous mobster who was considered to be so intelligent that he was able to feign insanity to throw the law off his trail. Or was he?

When the interview concluded and only the two agents remained, they looked at each and said as if on cue, "'The best poppa'? That was strange."

CHAPTER
THIRTY-FOUR

TEXAS/COLOMBIA
Early 1978–Early 1980

WHEN THE TELLER unlocked the front doors of the Denton bank at 9:00 a.m., she saw a familiar face waiting, Muscles Foster. He was in an apparent hurry and explained that he just needed to get into a bank box. He produced the key, and she took the box into a private room where he began transferring stacks of bills—$700,000 in all—into an oversized athletic bag he'd brought with him. Then he left as quickly as he'd entered.

A few days later, members of the joint task force and Texas law enforcement agents went to speak with Muscles regarding his involvement with the *Agnes Pauline*. Everywhere they went people told them the same story. "Muscles isn't here." "We haven't seen him for a few days." "No, he's not around. In fact, I've been trying to talk to him." He had disappeared, which was something he'd been known to do whenever he had a broken heart or trouble was chasing him.

So, the task force turned to questioning individuals who had agreed to cooperate with the investigation, while also having law enforcement check out his known haunts and associates in faraway states. Nothing turned up. But several friends did note that Muscles had always planned to go to Bolivia if things went bad with the drug-running business, since that country was known to deny extradition to the U.S. for anyone facing drug crimes.

⸻

RUPPEL AND GERDES sat in Tennessee cursing themselves for somehow forgetting that Muscles had access to the safe deposit box. They needed to have cash available at many locations across the country, and someone forgot to get the bank box key back from Muscles.

While they mourned the loss of desperately needed cash, Muscles sat alone in a dark air-conditioned lounge where he could be found nearly every afternoon sipping on cold tumbo cocktails.

On this particular day, two Bolivian police officers approached Muscles and explained that he needed to accompany them across town. Muscles cooperated but left with a look of defeat on his face. He knew they weren't going across town, and his days of freedom were circling the drain. He soon found himself on a plane headed back to the States under the guard of U.S. Marshals, fourteen months after he'd disappeared.

How the extradition occurred was never officially revealed. *Unofficially*, the word was that Special Agents had gone to Bolivia and presented the local police chief with a sizeable sum of money to nab Muscles and turn him over to U.S. agents at the airport. Regardless of how it happened, Muscles was finally in custody and would face his day in court.

CHAPTER
THIRTY-FIVE

TEXAS
1979–1980

THE GOVERNMENT'S case against the sixteen defendants related to the *Aggie* rested heavily on a statement Willis Judge Butler made to DEA agents that outlined five of the drug shipments that occurred between August 1976 and December 1978. He signed an agreement to tell the government everything he knew. Then at the trial in September 1979, it came to light that Butler had failed to tell the government about a time he drove 8,000 pounds of marijuana from a port in Louisiana to Colorado. This would add a sixth trip to the five around which the government had based its case. What else had Butler not told them about? This sixth trip was Butler's "baby," as it was the point at which he felt his position and power in the organization finally rose above Muscles.

Before a trial could even take place, the court appointed Dr. Lake Littlejohn to determine if Muscles was competent to stand trial. The psychiatrist said that due to "a great deal of deprivation" as a child that Muscles had "an intense need for dependency relationships," and had "deeply embedded feelings of isolation and loneliness."

When Muscles's case finally reached the courts, he didn't even spend his own money for legal representation. He was assigned a court-appointed lawyer, G. Brockett Irwin. Irwin used the insanity defense. Muscles's sister, Jo Ann Wells, told the jury how Muscles worked to help support his family beginning at the tender age of ten. He dropped out before high school but became a paratrooper, and after that began working for Rex Cauble. At times, he seemed detached from reality. So was it possible for him to be "insane" and also be a criminal mastermind? After all, Muscles had managed to plot how to get loans, use Rex's planes, store tons of marijuana, and transfer it across the country.

When asked by an attorney if Muscles was capable of carrying out the tasks of a drug operation such as organizing crews of people, securing storage locations, and planning details, his sister replied, "He can't organize, supervise, manage, or control himself, let alone a big enterprise." There was some truth to her claim, including a time when sixty-nine of Rex's cattle died because Muscles simply forgot about them. And Muscles was known to just disappear for weeks without being heard from. Yet at the same time he was the head of a dozen ranches that ran like clockwork.

Irwin's second witness, Muscles's psychologist Dr. Donald Whaley, agreed with Muscles's sister. He pointed out that Muscles's brain impairment led to an inability to think clearly or focus. The prosecution questioned whether someone with such a brain impairment could have the forethought to quickly obtain hundreds of thousands of dollars in cash and escape undetected to Bolivia. Irwin stated that, "Charles Elbert 'Muscles' Foster is no more a kingpin than he is a man possessed of muscles."

As if all this testimony wasn't enough to focus on, Ruppel's third trial was occurring in conjunction with Muscles's trial. Ruppel's lawyer, Robert Richie, painted Ruppel as the innocent victim of greedy drug kingpins, one of whom was Willis Judge Butler, the government's key witness. Ruppel's and Muscles's attorneys urged the jury to believe the objective friends who testified, rather than government witnesses such as Butler who were bargaining for leniency on their own behalf. But how was it possible for Ruppel to have had no knowledge of what was going on when he'd known Hawkins had been in prison for several years on drug-related charges?

The strategy worked for Muscles who, after an eight-day trial, was found not guilty by reason of insanity on eight counts of racketeering, conspiracy, and possession of marijuana. But not so for Ruppel. Judge Robert Parker sentenced the Tennessee millionaire to five years in prison and fined him $30,000 after he was convicted of one count of conspiracy to import and three counts of possession of marijuana with intent to distribute. It was, at the very least, better than the fifteen years he'd been sentenced to at his second trial, a sentence that was overturned when it was revealed that witnesses against him had made deals with the government for leniency.

Special Agent Fred Boff was sure of one thing, Muscles *was* pulling a "Vincent." Muscles was business smart and had an unparalleled knack for self-preservation. He drooled when he needed to show he was mentally incompetent, yet with a flip of a switch he could change into shrewd drug kingpin mode. He was playing everyone, even his psychologist.

CHAPTER THIRTY-SIX

NEW YORK/TEXAS
1979

FRED THRIVED on the days when the office was a beehive. Agents were in and out of Fred's office, and between the questions and constant phone calls (everyone he knew decided this was the day to pick his brain), the workload had swelled seemingly before his eyes. He was in the middle of a phone call when Hatch came in and sat stoically with perfect posture, occasionally reaching out to straighten one of Fred's haphazard piles that contained who knows what.

Had the situation been reversed, Fred would have plopped himself down and crossed his legs on Hatch's desk—something he'd actually done last week. Fred had known that Hatch was on an important call at the time so chose that moment to provide some good-natured and completely unnecessary needling. Hatch made desperate hand motions for Fred to put his feet down. Fred shrugged and made an I-don't-understand face then broke into a devilish grin. Hatch leaned over and shoved at Fred's foot. Fred responded again with a puzzled shrug. Then Hatch lobbed a crumbled-up wad of paper at Fred who caught it midair and in almost the same motion sent it sailing perfectly into the garbage can. But now, Hatch sat with attentive ears listening to one side of the conversation. It was one of those qualities that made him an exceptional investigator.

"Absolutely," Fred continued. "We will fly down... You said *Tuesday*? That's soon, but we will definitely be there Tuesday... I'll have Myrna in the travel office book it. He's not going to back out as soon as we get there, right? Hatch and I don't want to fly all the way for nothing."

At the sound of his name, the smile drained from Hatch's face. He mouthed *what* to Fred, and suddenly he was standing next to his partner straining to hear the person on the other line. Fred said his goodbyes and hung up.

"We're going back to Denton. The Old Man says he'll talk to us."

Travelling came with the job, but for eight months the two had been crisscrossing the southern part of the country investigating the purported drug ring. Hatch had put in for a day's leave on Wednesday, but disappointing family and cancelling plans came with the territory.

━━

THEY WERE MEETING on a warm afternoon at one of Rex's banks near Denton. Though not a town as well-known as other Texas destinations, Denton had a nostalgic charm, as well as a powerful feeling that came from being a flourishing community. Home to two former Miss Americas, Phyllis George and Shirley Cochran, the little city sat proudly in the shadow of Dallas.

It was here that Fred and Hatch got their first look at the self-made millionaire. Rex had requested the interview take place in an office at one of his banks. It seemed to be a rather thinly veiled attempt to get a home field advantage. The atmosphere in the room changed when Rex Cauble strode in, bringing a well-mannered yet arrogant charisma with him. He offered a hearty handshake and immediately made the agents feel welcome in this well-appointed conference room.

Dressed in a western suit complete with kerchief tie, cowboy hat, and boots, the outfit likely came courtesy of one of his exclusive Cutter Bill's Western Wear locations. The agents had a natural eye for detail. Rex's appearance was on the flashy side, yet nothing about his clothing would have warned them that each piece likely carried a price tag with four digits on it. Rex's southern manners wouldn't have allowed him to bring attention to his exclusive designer wear anyway. He was a man so financially well-endowed that the buttery-leather chairs and highly polished rosewood conference table that spanned the length of the room spoke for themselves.

Rex's attorney, Mel Bruder, dramatically placed a briefcase on the table, completed curt introductions, and sat next to his client. Bruder was not as well-dressed as the wealthy man next to him, but his deep-set eyes and sideburns completed this picture of a savvy attorney ready to pounce on anyone who might dare provoke his client.

Fred and Hatch's plan was to let Rex do most of the talking; thereby, using The Old Man's ego to give them passages into his life. At the same time, the agents would be revealing as little information as possible about where the investigation was heading.

Fred began. "You understand that we are investigating an expansive drug distribution organization, and your name has come up by several people who have been indicted in this case. We would like to give you the opportunity to address what you know about this."

Rex's attorney turned to him with a nod indicating that it was okay to answer, but Rex wasn't waiting for anyone's permission. He'd already launched into his dialogue. Reading between the lines, Fred knew Rex was not one to be caught off guard. He'd likely already pressed his attorney for clear parameters regarding what he would and would not answer.

Rex leaned back in his chair casually, removed his black custom cowboy hat, and folded his arms across his chest. "I have a *lot* of people working for me. I am a busy man and not around much. I don't know of and certainly cannot control the shenanigans that some of my employees and hired hands get themselves mixed up in." He shrugged nonchalantly. His expression of unconcern explained that he was pompous enough to think that with this one brief statement, he had clearly explained away any liability he might have.

"So, Mr. Cauble," Hatch began, flipping open a manila folder and running a finger down a page of numbers, "do you think it's typical for a business to be making frequent cash deposits of $250,000?"

Rex didn't squirm or move so much as a muscle. "Oh, I do a lot of business in cash. Cash don't bounce. I do cattle deals quite often."

Rex was likely unaware of information the agents had uncovered that at one of Rex's banks, he was on a list of businesses that were exempt from having cash deposits above $10,000 reported to the IRS. "I see. Then it should not be too difficult to match up the deposits with a matching receipt for the sale of cattle. It will all line up legally, I presume?" But it did not line up and already Rex's polished story was starting to crack and falter.

For the next hour, The Old Man and his attorney answered with the same brief, well-rehearsed answers. The tone was civil yet sharp-edged from both sides of the table. Rex managed to fit in the irrelevant fact that he'd played in the first World Series of Poker in Las Vegas. At the end of the interview, Fred handed Rex a business card. "Mr. Cauble, call me anytime you want."

And The Old Man did call.

REX CAUBLE'S MONEY, connections, and power were not enough to get him off the legal hook. But Rex was not indicted until August 7, 1981, after trials for some of the other suspects had wrapped up. The indictments gave the government nearly free reign to examine all of Rex's holdings, including his ranches and Cutter Bill stores. Special Agent George Redden testified that one of the DEA's primary objectives was to set up a pyramid in which lower-level players in the drug ring would testify against those above them and so on, until the key players were left to testify against Rex in hopes of getting lighter sentences. The FBI and DEA spent three years gathering evidence before The Old Man went to trial on January 11, 1982.

Rex was indicted on ten counts including violation of banking laws and causing the importation of marijuana into the U.S. Prosecutors said Rex got involved because Cauble Enterprises was in financial trouble. When the smuggling was occurring, a lot of cash was deposited into Cauble Enterprises accounts. Rex's accountant, Carolyn McDonnel, was not able to find names, addresses, or telephone numbers of nine people who allegedly bought cattle from Cauble and paid in cash. It didn't look good. Further casting doubt on Cauble's innocence, the controller of his company quit after the *Aggie* incident and after telling Cauble he would not authorize the cash sale of cattle without proof. Prosecutors said Rex used his position at a bank to get loans for Muscles.

Some of Rex's associates such as James Holland said Rex was not aware his property was being used in the marijuana operation. Cauble rarely went to the ranches and preferred his offices in Denton. Holland claimed that Muscles had them more worried about what would happen if Rex Cauble found out what was going on than if the police caught them.

One of the shrimp boat pilots, Robert Hamm, testified that Cauble knew nothing about the marijuana and that it was Muscles who gave the orders for the many loads Hamm brought from Colombia. Rex secured several notable character witnesses including Ruth Carter Stapleton, an evangelist and sister of President Jimmy Carter

Muscles defended him as well. "Rex Cauble is not guilty of what he's been charged with," Muscles told U.S. District Judge William Steger in 1984. "And (if) you're going to sentence a man today, you should be sentencing this man sitting in this chair because I am the guilty man."

Steger responded, "Yes, but a jury found you insane, Mr. Foster."

"Well, that might be true, sir. But I don't think I'm any more insane than anybody here… As God is my witness, this man is not guilty of what he's charged with."

Though a few people gave statements to help The Old Man out, there were too many questionable transactions involving large amounts of cash. And others involved in the operation spoke out against him. Hawkins, one of the big players, testified against Rex in hopes of getting a lighter sentence, and supposedly had a deal that they would not prosecute his wife, Karen, if he testified. William McKesson, one of Rex's pilots, testified that Muscles said Rex knew about the operation but didn't ask detailed questions. Many presented evidence showing Rex knew exactly what was going on. Others felt he turned a blind eye, and it was willful ignorance.

FRED NEVER DETERMINED EXACTLY why Rex Cauble chose to call him off and on after their meetings in Texas. It seemed odd since Fred had worked diligently to get The Old Man convicted of various crimes. It could have been that he truly liked Fred's blunt and honest personality. Likewise, it was well known that Rex enjoyed having friendly relationships with lawmen. Or maybe he thought that if he stayed on good terms with Fred that the agent might testify favorably in any future legal mishaps. He usually knew how to work his way into someone's life if that's where he decided he wanted to be.

"Hello, Fred! You been able to have any fun, or do they have you out arresting bad guys day and night?" Rex chuckled. Their phone conversations were always casual guy talk, and Rex did not shy away from salty banter.

"Rex, someone told me that when you were traveling around, you have a hooker on salary who's always with you?"

Rex answered rather proudly. "There might be a few false rumors floating around out there about me, but what you heard is true. You're a young man, Fred, but when you're my age you have to remember the old saying, 'If you don't use it, you'll lose it.'"

Both men laughed at that one. And so, Fred spoke with The Old Man and even received Christmas cards from the popular Texas millionaire.

Fred had mixed feelings about whether or not Rex was guilty. He was very convincing during the interviews. Many people believed Rex had been duped. He was generous to a fault and often loaned money without asking much about why the person needed it. Was he blinded by his dysfunctional relationship with Muscles? Yet, there was a lot of evidence against him. "I don't know. It makes me wonder," was Fred's final summary.

CHAPTER
THIRTY-SEVEN

NEW YORK
1980s

THE DEEP AND tangled web of drug running and violence perpetrated by what was dubbed the Cowboy Mafia had slowly wound down. Fred, Hatch, Redden, and the rest of the task force were big factors in securing evidence that led to dozens of people being indicted. Working life eventually fell back into its old routine for Fred, Hatch, and many others who'd played a part in bringing justice.

As Fred approached retirement, he reflected on the memories of his favorite partner, Hatch. One memory that occurred when the massive drug case was reaching its climax often caused him to suddenly laugh out loud.

As the massive drug case reached its climax, Fred and Hatch were on the go continually with more work than twenty-four hours in a day would allow. And as if there wasn't enough stress with investigating the DEA's biggest drug case to date, Fred now found himself squished —nearly squished cheek-to-cheek—next to Hatch, their faces touching. They had been driving on the highway in their government car when a fully loaded semitruck went out of control and tipped over onto their vehicle, smashing it like an accordion. They were lucky to be alive.

The doors were crushed, and a rescue crew was on its way to cut them out. In typical Hatch fashion, he turned the situation into something humorous. He nuzzled his nose in Fred's hair and breathed in deeply. "You smell *so* good!"

Fred tried to shrug him away, but he could barely move. "What the hell are you doing?"

Hatch snuggled again, knowing his wit was getting to Fred. "Did anyone ever tell you you have bedroom eyes? You ever been kissed by a black guy before?"

Fred groaned. It was typical Hatch to take this near-death experience and inject comedy into it. Fred could hear his heart pounding rapidly beneath his chest, and yet here was Hatch calm as could be and cracking jokes. Fred called to the policeman standing outside the car. "Hey, I can't reach my gun. Can you hand me yours, so I can shoot this jackass in here?"

<hr />

WHEN FRED RETIRED and stepped away from the job he loved, Ginger could finally sleep more peacefully at night. Fred had only two regrets from his years as a Special Agent. The most important was the time he lost from being away from his family. As his father had always taught him, live life every day the best you can and enjoy it as much as possible, because today is one thing we can never replace, and the other thing is yesterday. Although he knew that was true, now in retirement he planned to make up for as much lost time as possible.

The other regret had less impact on his life and more on his psyche. He'd had the best job in the world as a Special Agent. The work was extremely interesting, exciting, and rewarding when it came to his own self-image. He traveled to many places he wouldn't have otherwise seen, and interacted with people of all backgrounds. He was proud of what he'd accomplished, and he couldn't quite place his finger on where the regret was coming from until the day he ran into a former coworker. They discussed the good ol' days, and warm memories bubbled to the surface. Fred thought back to when he had initially applied for a job. He had done so with thousands of others. Then he made the first cut and endured an eighteen-month invasive background investigation that delved into every aspect of his life. From that, he emerged with maybe forty or fifty others who made it to the training academy where they went through months of rigorous physical, academic, mental, and emotional testing. And then "that day" arrived: he was handed a gun, a badge, and a small leather case with his credentials that read *Special Agent*. And indeed, he felt very special. But once he retired, that feeling of being someone extraordinary started to fade. He was no longer part of the prestigious ether that bound him together in a unique camaraderie with other Special Agents."

Hatch, perhaps the finest human being he had ever known, and the man Fred loved like a brother, remained on the job continuing to be one of the DEA's top Special Agents and most committed employees. Special Agents were assigned to most cases, but they could also volunteer for assignments that played to their strengths or maybe simply drew their interest. It was one such opportunity in early 1989 that caused Hatch to accept an undercover assignment that involved him infiltrating the drug network of one of New York's five organized crime families. Ever the gung-ho agent, Hatch asked his supervisor about the assignment and was told, "We have credible information about several members within the Gambino family. These people are distributing large amounts of cocaine, and we need a UC to work the case."

There was no hesitation before Hatch accepted the assignment. It was simply who he was...fearless. Now with seventeen years under his belt as a DEA agent, he dove into the risky assignments with the same perfectionism and professionalism he did with every case every single time. Hatch's attention to detail and ability to perform under pressure were second to no one. Such qualities were vital to anyone going undercover, to minimize the chance of slipping up and even possibly being exposed as an agent. He familiarized himself with every detail received from the reliable informant.

Partway through the investigation, after several preliminary meetings, Hatch arranged yet another meeting with the main target. Hatch directed the surveillance agents to not get too close because "there's no

weigh the enjoyment and satisfaction I got from the job against all the turmoil and sacrifices it caused my wife and kids, I'm not sure whether I'd do it again." He paused in thoughtful contemplation with the mature eyes of a seventy-eight-year-old man who has gained the ability to flesh out insights he missed as a young and busy father and husband. "I guess, in the end, you can't live your life again, so you hope you did what you did for the right reasons. Sadly, it's a question I know I'll never really be able to answer."

EPILOGUE

SPECIAL AGENTS FRED BOFF, EVERETT "HATCH" Hatcher, and the other federal and state law enforcement teams were looking for "The Big One." Who was the main kingpin of the Cowboy Mafia? The DEA's plan was to start with the lower-level participants of the operation who would likely get immunity for testifying against the people at the middle level. The people at the middle level would get a deal or reduced sentence for testifying against The Big One. But it turned out that there was not just a single Big One. The operation was too widespread and elaborate. Based on their ownership of shrimp boats to import drugs, their ability to transport and store drugs, their ability to organize portions of the drug ring, or having the wealth to help finance the operations, there ended up being six Big Ones: Willis Judge Butler, John Ruppel, Carlos Gerdes, Raymond Hawkins, Charles "Muscles" Foster, and Rex Cauble.

A key factor in breaking the Cowboy Mafia was the information provided by Ronnie Ray. Fred Boff found Ronnie Ray to be an informant who was not only extremely valuable, based on his familiarity with the drug ring, but was also likeable and trustworthy—a rarity among the criminals he worked with. Ronnie Ray became an "invisible informant" who was granted immunity for the information he knew, and his identity was protected to every extent possible. When the dust settled on the trials, Ronnie Ray simply faded off. Those who had worked with him lost track of his whereabouts. Fred's hope was that Ronnie Ray learned valuable lessons about the criminal life and decided to stay on the straight and narrow.

TRIALS AND VERDICTS

The Six Big Ones

Willis Judge Butler, 42, Mesquite, TX—The state's key witness during the *Aggie* trial. He was a defendant until he agreed to testify under a plea bargain. He died May 18, 1981, at age 44 from an apparent suicide.

Rex Cauble, 70, Denton, TX—Convicted on charges of financing a smuggling ring. There were ten counts including: Rex Cauble and Cauble Enterprises conspired to carry out racketeering activity and conspiring to smuggle 212,000 pounds of high-grade marijuana. He was found guilty of embezzling more than $147,000 from the Western State Bank of Denton and the South Main Bank of Houston. He was sentenced to five years in prison on each count, to be served concurrently, and directed to surrender his 31% interest in Cauble Enterprises (ranching, steel, and oil companies; a Western wear store; and more, said to be worth $75 million–$80 million). At the time, it was the largest seizure of assets under the Racketeer Influenced and Corrupt Organizations (RICO) Act. Although the government seized Cauble's assets, it left his wife Josephine and son, Lewis, their portion of the family empire.

Rex entered prison in 1982 and was released in 1987 (forty-one months later) from the "Big Fish" La Tuna Federal Correctional Institution in Texas. Josephine and Rex had not had a real marriage for years, and upon his release from prison they divorced. He was nearly broke and figured he'd be awarded half of his wife's fortune. The judge disagreed and said that Rex had no claim to Josephine's portion of the company. Rex remarried and lived in a modest high-rise apartment in Dallas, which he was able to afford due to the $7,700 a month Josephine was court ordered to pay him. Rex continued making occasional calls and sending Christmas cards to Special Agent Fred Boff throughout the years, and once met him in a New York City restaurant where they had a lobster dinner. For the rest of his life, Cauble claimed he was innocent.

He died on June 23, 2003, in Oklahoma, at the age of 89.

Charles Elbert "Muscles" Foster, 50, Denton, TX—Muscles pled innocent by reason of insanity. After an eight-day trial and seven and a half hours of deliberation, he was found not guilty on all eight counts of racketeering, conspiracy, and possession of marijuana charges. He thanked the judge for a fair trial. So, Muscles using an insanity plea, walked free. The insanity ploy probably worked due to his past mental health record of suicide attempts, wandering away from his normal life for weeks on end, memory loss, and a history of electric shock treatments. Special Agent Fred Boff commented, "Give ol' Muscles and his lawyers credit for pulling off a defense that worked. I still believe it was mostly an act on Muscles's part. He played the crazy cards well."

On July 5, 1989, Muscles was discovered dead in a Paris, Texas, motel room. He was sixty years old.

Carlos Gerdes (AKA Carlos San Ramen), Pigeon Forge and Newport, TN—Former owner of the Colonial House Motel and Restaurant. Pled guilty to racketeering charges. Sentenced to twenty years and served twelve years. Also fined $110,000.

Raymond Eugene Hawkins, Denton, TX (Cherokee Ranch)— Convicted on all counts: one for conspiracy and five related drug smuggling charges. He pled guilty to one drug charge with the others dismissed in exchange for testimony against Cauble.

John Ruppel, 60, Gatlinburg, TN—Made a fortune in his land development businesses. His first trial ended in a mistrial. At the next trial he was found guilty of seven counts including conspiracy to

smuggle 73½ tons of marijuana into the U.S., three counts of possession of marijuana with intent to distribute, and being an organizer in a
continuing criminal enterprise. He was sentenced to five years in
prison and fined $30,000. He appealed. After three trials, Ruppel was
acquitted of racketeering charges and operating a continuing criminal
enterprise. These charges could have led to life imprisonment and
forfeiture of his property. He was found guilty of four drug-related
charges: conspiracy to violate federal drug laws and three counts of
possession of marijuana. During his trials, Muscles was fingered as the
kingpin.

Following is a list of other primary people involved with the Cowboy
Mafia but at a lower level.

Jimmy Lee Brooks, 33, Baton Rouge, LA—Charges of conspiracy to
possess with intent to distribute marijuana were dismissed.

Elmer Douglas Culver Jr., 27, Crossville, TN—Pled guilty to smuggling marijuana aboard the trawler *Agnes Pauline*. Sentenced to three
years and another three years to run concurrently. Also fined $10,000.

Gloria Jean Davis, 30, Denton TX—Charges of conspiracy to
possess with intent to distribute marijuana were dismissed.

Dayton Bud Eans Jr., 29, Bouch Springs, TX—Charges of
conspiracy to possess with intent to distribute marijuana were
dismissed.

Les Wallick Fuller, 49, Arbrey, TX—He was aboard a plane that
disappeared May 7, 1980. The twin-engine six-passenger Grumman
Cougar apparently flew into a thunderstorm and crashed while on a
flight from Port Isabel to Dallas. Fuller was the pilot. At the time, he
was free on bond pending an appeal of a six-month prison term for
marijuana smuggling. At first only three bodies were found. Some
authorities suspected that he staged the crash and was still alive.
However, his badly decomposed body was later recovered.

Robert Hamm, 34, Florida—Admitted paying $148,000 for the
Monkey. He became a government witness and described how the drug
runners would use secret signals by light to make the exchange with

the suppliers in Colombia. They used code words to identify each other. It took them 2½ hours to unload 45,000 pounds of marijuana in 50-pound bales and 1½ weeks to get the bales distributed around the country.

Harold F. Hannon, 37 (employee of Sneed Sr. shipbuilding firm)—Convicted on all counts. Six years in prison, a fine of $25,000, and a 3-year parole.

Beth Holland, Sevierville, TN—Acquitted on all counts.

James "Jamie" Holland, 49 (rancher), Sevierville, TN—Convicted and sentenced to 15 years on smuggling. Also a 5-year sentence to run concurrently, fined $55,000, and a 6-year parole.

James Monroe Loungendyke, Jr., 47, Key Largo, FL—Charges of conspiracy to possess with intent to distribute marijuana were dismissed.

Holly Jean Mosel, 24, Miami, FL—Charges of conspiracy to possess with intent to distribute marijuana were dismissed.

Bryant O'Neal (AKA Joseph Gosnell, an employee of Sneed Sr. shipbuilding firm)—Convicted on all counts. 6 years in prison, $25,000 fine, and 3-year parole.

Randolph L. Peyton, 39, Miami, FL—Charges of conspiracy to possess with intent to distribute marijuana were dismissed.

Ronald Spencer Ray—Deleted from the list of defendants without explanation at the September 20, 1979, federal drug conspiracy trial in Beaumont, TX.

Clyde Sneed (nephew of Martin Sneed Sr.)—Found guilty on one of three counts. Three years in prison, $10,000 fine, and 2-year parole.

Donald Sneed—Deleted from the list of defendants without explanation at the September 20, 1979, federal drug conspiracy trial in Beaumont, TX.

Martin Marion Sneed, Jr., Orange, TX—Found guilty on two of three counts. Sentenced to 5 years in prison, a fine of $15,000, and a 3-year parole.

Martin Sneed, Sr., (shipbuilder), Orange, TX—Found guilty on seven of the eight counts including continuing criminal enterprise. Sentenced to 12 years in prison, a $55,000 fine, and 2-year parole.

Clifford Swier (employee of Martin Sneed Sr.)—Convicted on all counts except for conspiracy. Sentenced to 3 years in prison, a $10,000 fine and a 2-year parole.

Maurice Merle Sythe, Groves, TX—Charges of conspiracy to possess with intent to distribute marijuana were dismissed.

Charles Talkington, 41 (Cauble's ranch hand)—Cooperated with the federal government after pleading guilty to one drug count. Sentenced to 2 years for smuggling.

Myriene Vice (employee of Martin Sneed Sr.)—Taken into custody but not indicted.

Larry Dale Washington, 31, Bouch Springs, TX—Witness for the prosecution; testified that marijuana was stored on Cauble-owned ranches and warehouses.

James Eddie Wimberly (brother of Thomas and both in the horse training business)—Acquitted on all counts.

Thomas T. Wimberly, 39, Vinton, LA—Convicted on two of three counts (not conspiracy). 6 years in prison, fines of $25,000, and 4-year parole.

Sandy Creek (Cowboy Mafia) Drug and Murder Trials

When the *Gunsmoke* steamed into Sandy Creek, it was just one of the many shipping ventures that fell under what would become known as the Cowboy Mafia. The trials got messy for the Sandy Creek drug smuggling ring and murders. One journalist said it led "to a tangle of state and federal legal actions so complex that even those who have followed the case for months have trouble keeping the characters straight." There was public outcry when it was reported that a Tallahassee, Florida, FBI agent, Donald Baldwin, knew about the drugs coming into the Florida coast. The big question was why something wasn't done about it before four innocent people were executed.

Although all eight defendants admitted they were part of the Sandy Creek smuggling ring, the defense claimed that none of them were guilty due to the whole scheme being entrapment. They pointed out that Bobby Joe Vines, who owned the aluminum boats used to ferry the marijuana to shore, had been working secretly with FBI agent Baldwin. It was said that Baldwin was trying to coordinate a huge drug bust so he could make the arrests and take credit for himself and the FBI.

During a month of testimony, the defense painted Vines as an FBI informant who tempted citizens who would have otherwise not broken the law into participating in a drug ring with promises of enormous sums of money for little work.

Not so, the prosecution countered. Vines, they claimed, had double-crossed the FBI by giving Baldwin false or misleading information about the smuggling ring and playing out the whole operation under Baldwin's nose without his knowledge. Vines had never been paid more than $50, and that had been in 1976. After that he was told the FBI would no longer be needing his services as an informant, and this was long before the Sandy Creek murders.

There was a lot of finger-pointing during the trial. When prosecutors tried to pin the label of professional drug smuggler on Steven Lukefahr, he replied that he wasn't sure how the feds defined a professional, but by his viewpoint a professional is someone who walks away with $300,000 and wears $400 suits purchased with money received from the FBI. He was referring, of course, to Bobby Joe Vines, who had inked a deal enabling him to walk away from any accountability.

The Sandy Creek drug smuggling operation, which at first glance had seemed so well organized, quickly fell apart. David Capo, David Goodwin, his brother, and three others had arranged for twenty tons of pot to be hauled from Colombia to Sandy Creek via the *Gunsmoke.*

Once it arrived, they would be turning the rest of the operation over to Vines who had arranged for the unloading, moving, and storage of the marijuana. He'd hired David and Christopher Goodwin, Walter Steinhorst, and Lloyd Woods who formed one group. Capo hired the three Lukefahr brothers whom he knew to be professional drug smugglers. Each group was assigned its own specific tasks the night the marijuana arrived.

The first problem was on January 22, 1977, when the *Gunsmoke* ran out of gas. The next night, the shrimper arrived as expected, but then four innocent friends drove up on the drug smugglers, caught them red-handed, and this resulted in their murders. After the first shooting occurred on the beach, the whole plan began to unravel. The crew of the *Gunsmoke* took off and eventually purposely sank the shrimper with half the marijuana still onboard, and another group scuttled their aluminum boat, which resulted in dozens of bales of marijuana to be seen bobbing like corks around the bay the following morning. Some of the smugglers took off with the captives to complete the executions. All of the failures involving the Sandy Creek smuggling operation helped shine another light on the Cowboy Mafia. Sandy Creek gave the DEA vital information to piece together the widespread drug operation.

After eight hours of testimony, the jury made its decisions on the drug smuggling charges in late February 1978. The four local "boys" who were hired by Vines were acquitted: Walter Steinhorst, Christopher and David Goodwin, and Lloyd Woods. This was due to the jury feeling that it was entrapment since Vines was working secretly with an FBI agent. Found guilty were David, Thomas and Steven Lukefahr, and David Capo. They had not been hired by Vines. Edwin Marger, the attorney for the three Lukefahr brothers stated that it was the first case he'd lost in federal court in twenty-five years and would appeal.

Later, State Attorney Ed Austin announced that the Florida Department of Criminal Law Enforcement should be "absolved officially of any wrongdoing." Austin had been in charge of the state's investigation into allegations that the FBI and other agencies were partly liable for the "Sinkhole Murders." They determined that agent Baldwin had been careless in how he had used the information received from Vines, but did not have knowledge to have stopped the operation or the murders. He was, they admitted, "out of his field of expertise," since the FBI does not typically handle drug cases, which takes intricate training. As far as FBI agent Baldwin's accountability for knowing about the smuggling, it was turned over to his superiors to decide internally and confidentially if there would be disciplinary action or not.

In late April of 1978, Walter Steinhorst, David Capo, Lloyd Woods, and David Goodwin went to trial for the murder of the four people who innocently came upon the Sandy Creek drug smuggling. At Steinhorst's trial, Evelyn McAdams, the mother of the two slain sisters, got up on the stand to testify, but broke down in tears upon seeing the photos of her daughters. Then Faye Sims, wife of murder victim Harold Sims, took the stand, but she too broke down.

The defense ruffled some feathers by suggesting that the four murder victims had perhaps gone down there to hijack the marijuana and in doing so purposely started a confrontation. Steinhorst's lawyer suggested his client was an outsider compared to the others who had likely banded together and agreed to all tell the same story that pointed to Steinhorst as the guilty party.

Vines admitted he told Steinhorst, "I don't care what anyone tells you, you stop us from getting shot in the back and you protect this drug shipment." This was in relation to Steinhorst being the guard of the operation and the one with the firearms in hand when the first of the four was shot in his pickup as it arrived at the beach.

Steinhorst was convicted on four counts of first-degree murder. The first murder was at the beach, and the other was the execution-style killing of the three people at the sinkhole. He was also guilty of aiding and abetting in their kidnapping, which ended in murder. The jury was further shocked when it was revealed Steinhorst told a friend that it was unfortunate that the girls had to be killed since one of them "had such cute breasts." The jury recommended death for three of the counts and a life sentence for the fourth.

The following people were involved in the Sandy Creek drug operation. (Ages are given at the time of the Sandy Creek indictments in 1977.)

Thomas Bruce Byerly, 28 (part of the crew unloading at Sandy Beach)—Pleaded guilty to felony possession of marijuana. Byerly had been previously indicted in 1975 for marijuana-related charges in an unrelated case. Charges were dropped in exchange for testimony.

David Floyd Capo, 29 (a fisherman) Cortez—Guilty of conspiracy to smuggle marijuana and possession of the drug with intent to distribute. 4 years in prison on one count and 3 years on the other to be served concurrently, $20,000 fine, 2 years special parole to follow.

Initially charged with third-degree murder but the charge was dropped. He testified in Steinhorst's trial after receiving immunity.

Floyd Farrell "Bubba" Capo, 45 (a fisherman) Horseshoe Beach—Charges of conspiracy to import nearly forty tons of marijuana on the *Gunsmoke* were dropped due to insufficient evidence. When he was arrested, the citizens in the tiny Horseshoe Beach hamlet were shocked that their generous and well-liked neighbor had an alter-ego. They were evidently unaware that he'd been convicted for smuggling marijuana several years prior.

William Hunt Epperson, Jr., 35, Tallahassee—Plea bargained, identified eight of the defendants, and gave information about the drug ring Epperson also testified that he'd received death threats that scared him to the point that he wanted to change his guilty plea and renege on his agreement to testify for the government. William did testify against the eight. William was sentenced to 5 years in prison with all but 4 months suspended.

Peter Van Slyke Estrup, 35 (Sarasota ship builder, captain. and owner of the *Gunsmoke*, but no evidence he was there the night of the murders), Bradenton—Charged with first-degree murder, charges were dropped due to insufficient evidence. He had purchased the shrimping trawler the previous year and instructed the boat broker not to bother putting shrimp nets on it.

Christopher Dale Goodwin, 25 (welder for Nuclear Power Products), Panama City—Acquitted of marijuana conspiracy and possession charges (hired by Vines) in exchange for grand jury testimony.

David Monroe Goodwin, 30 (former stock handler at Tyndall Air Force Base), Merritt Island—Acquitted of marijuana conspiracy and possession charges (hired by Vines), convicted of first-degree murder, and sentenced to death. He was found guilty of first-degree murder due to being instrumental in kidnappings that led to the murders. In 1981, he received a vacated judgment for the death sentence. On May 2, 2017, he left the Everglades Correctional Institute in Miami at age 70, having been granted parole.

Charles Hughes, 32, Seven Mile, Ohio—Was on the FBI's most wanted list. He was found four years later living in Myrtle, Mississippi, working as a mechanic and going by the name George Hacker.

Myrtle residents were shocked as the courteous and friendly Hughes was a popular resident of the town. Once apprehended he was found guilty of the shooting death of Harold Sims. One person testified that Hughes commented the night of the murders that the witnesses had to die to protect the drug business. There was a mistrial on the other first-degree murder counts. Before his retrial, he pleaded guilty in a plea agreement to 3 reduced counts of second-degree murder. If he'd gone to trial on first-degree murder charges he could have been sentenced to death by electric chair. He was sentenced to three 15-year terms to be served consecutively. He ultimately served only 5 years in prison due to being paroled for good behavior.

Steven Buford Long, 29 (worked at a Panama City paper mill), Panama City—Helped pilot the *Gunsmoke*. U.S. District Court Judge William Stafford would not allow Long to testify that Peter Van Estrup was the captain of the *Gunsmoke*, due to it being determined that the way Long identified Van Estrup was tainted. Long admitted he helped choose the landing site for the *Gunsmoke* and guided in steering the boat to Sandy Creek from the Gulf of Mexico. Long was granted immunity in exchange for grand jury testimony.

David Lee Lukefahr, 42, St. Petersburg—Guilty of conspiracy to smuggle marijuana and possession of the drug with intent to distribute. David and his brothers, Thomas and Steven, were already serving a state prison sentence in Louisiana for drug smuggling at the time of their trial in Florida. David was sentenced to 5 years for each of the two counts against him to be served concurrently but independently of the Louisiana charges. David's attorney requested that his client be given special consideration since his wife recently passed away, and he had two children. The judge did not agree to this.

Steven Dale Lukefahr, 28, St. Petersburg—Guilty of conspiracy to smuggle marijuana and possession of the drug with intent to distribute. He was sentenced to 5 years for each of the two counts against him to be served concurrently but independently of the Louisiana charges.

Thomas Paul Lukefahr (AKA Thomas James Davison), 32, Jacksonville—Guilty of conspiracy to smuggle marijuana and possession of the drug with intent to distribute. He was sentenced to 5 years for each of the two counts against him to be served concurrently. He and Steven were then sent to Louisiana to serve the remainder of their prison sentences.

John Davis Mitchell, 29, Tallahassee—Plea bargained and testified against others along with Epperson. Sentenced to 5 years with all but a six-month jail sentence suspended. Directed to pay back the federal government for his court-appointed lawyer.

Raymond Parker, 27 (unloaded marijuana at Sandy Creek— Pleaded guilty of 2 misdemeanor charges of conspiracy to possess marijuana and possession of marijuana.

Walter Gale Steinhorst, 47, Live Oak—Charged with three murders, convicted of first-degree murder and sentenced to death, acquitted of marijuana conspiracy and possession charges. He was scheduled for execution in 1986, and one week before the scheduled death by electric chair, he was granted a stay. In 1997, he tried to claim that Charles Hughes shot the other three people at the sinkhole. He also asserted that the four people in the truck knew about the drug shipment, and that Harold Sims had tried to kill him in order to steal the pot. It was considered an unfounded claim with no evidence to support it. He died in prison in 1999 at the age of 68 after suffering several strokes and spending his last few years nearly blind and unable to walk.

Bobby Joe Vines, 40 (bartender). Tallahassee—Possible FBI informant. Given immunity for his testimony about the Sinkhole Murders.

Lloyd Andrew Woods, 25, Orlando—Charged with first-degree murder, acquitted of marijuana conspiracy and possession charges (hired by Vines).

When the drug runners sunk the *Gunsmoke*, it settled on the bottom of the ocean, and over the years strong currents did not break up the shrimper. The boat remains there today and is a popular place for scuba divers to explore, especially due to its ominous reputation.

CITATIONS

Chapter 13: "When we were bringing him up...he was glad we had found him." (*Tallahassee Democrat*, August 9, 1977, page 1 by Michael Whiteley "Murky water held secret").

Chapter 35: "a great deal of deprivation" "an intense need for dependency relationships" "deeply embedded feelings of isolation and loneliness." (*The Marshall News Messenger*, June 1, 1980, page 2 by Kevin Walter "Marshall psychiatrist says drug defendant could not be feeble-minded and organizer").

Chapter 35: "He can't organize, supervise...let alone a big enterprise." (*Longview News-Journal*, June 4, 1980, page 3 "Foster innocent Ruppel found guilty on 4 federal counts" by James Cullen).

Chapter 35: "Charles Elbert Muscles...a man possessed of muscles." (*Kilgore News Herald*, May 25, 1980. AP, page 6A).

Chapter 36: "Rex Cauble is not guilty of what he's been charged with" "And (if) you're going to sentence a man...sitting in this chair because I am the guilty man." "Yes, but a jury found you insane, Mr. Foster." "Well, that might be true...this man is not guilty of what he's charged with. (*Fort Worth Star-Telegram*, April 30, 1989, page 1 "Money and passion" by Barry Shlachter).

Trials and Verdicts: "had such cute breast(s)". and "I don't care what anyone tells you." (*Pensacola News* Journal May 3, 1978, p. 2 "Jones: Defendant Guilty in All Sinkhole Murders").

Trials and Verdicts: "to a tangle of state and federal legal actions so...have trouble keeping the characters straight" (*The Miami Herald*, April 24, 1978, page 92 "Sandy Creek Trials Begin 15 Months After Four Died).

━━━

Albertsons, Mike. "The Case of the Sinkhole Murders," *Pensacola News Journal*, January 29, 1978, 1,https://www.newspapers.com/image/265289093/?terms=The%20case%20of%20the%20sinkhole%20murders&match=1.

AP, "19 arrested in pot-smuggling," *Corpus Christi Times*, May 3, 1979, 11, https://www.newspapers.com/image/759420091/?terms=19%20arrested%20&match=1.

AP, "Body May be smuggler's," *Fort Worth Star-Telegram*, May 20, 1980, 10-B, https://www.newspapers.com/image/634957690/?terms=Body%20May%20be%20smugglers&match=1.

AP, "Denton man says he unloaded pot," *Fort Worth Star-Telegram*, September 13, 1979, 22, https://www.newspapers.com/image/634923773/?terms=Denton%20man%20unloaded%20pot&match=1.

AP, "Hughes pleads guilty to murder at Sandy Creek," *Tallahassee Democrat*, May 18, 1982, 13, https://www.newspapers.com/image/246038651/?terms=%22Charles%20Hughes%22%20sentenced%20Sandy%20creek&match=1.

AP, "Jurors convict nine of smuggling plot," *Wichita Falls Times*, September 23,1979, 3, https://www.newspapers.com/image/781468002/?terms=Jurors%20convict%209&match=1.

AP, "Key drug trial witness will testify," *The Paris News*, September 18, 1979, 3, https://www.newspapers.com/image/9773733/?terms=Key%20drug%20trial%20witness%20&match=1.

AP, "Killer claims accomplice shot three of four victims," *Florida Today*, August 6, 1997, 15, https://www.newspapers.com/image/

174548214/?terms=Killer%20claims%20accomplice%20shot%20three&
match=1.

AP, "Murder trial jury recesses after intense closing cases," *News-Press*, May 3, 1978, 11, https://www.newspapers.com/image/
213100269/?terms=Murder%20trial%20jury%20recesses&match=1.

AP, "Pot Trial Features Millionaire," *Victoria Advocate*, February
17,1980, 7, https://www.newspapers.com/image/436920521/?terms=
Pot%20trial%20features%20millionaire&match=1.

AP, "Prosecution: Guard For Pot Smugglers Killed an Intruder " *The
Miami Herald*, April 28, 1978, 13-D, https://www.newspapers.com/
image/627428937/?terms=%22Walter%20Steinhorst%22&match=1.

AP, "Prosecution rests case in 'Cowboy Mafia' trial," *The Galveston
Daily News*, January 22, 1982, 10, https://www.newspapers.com/
image/16692751/?terms=Prosecution%20rests%20case%20&match=1.

AP, "State's witness Butler in cross-examination," *San Angelo Standard Times*, September 18, 1979, 2, https://www.newspapers.com/
image/781802831/?terms=State%27s%20witness%20butler&match=1.

Charles Foster, obituary, *Paris News* (Paris, TX), 6 July,1989 page 2,
https://www.newspapers.com/image/5863948/?article=0c8a2186-
1e29-4064-877c-96f9642beb51.

Connor Jr., George and Watson, Margaret, "Witness Claims Cauble
Received $125,000," January 13, 1982, 1, 5, https://www.newspapers.
com/image/588780736/?terms=Cauble&match=1.

Cox Newspapers Wire Service, "24 Indicted After Narcotics Traffic
Investigation" *The Palm Beach Post*, May 3, 1979, C-3, https://www.
newspapers.com/image/134903423/?terms=24%20indicted%20nar
cotics%20&match=1.

Effron, Seth. "4 guilty, 4 innocent in smuggling trial," *Tallahassee
Democrat*, February 25,1978, https://www.newspapers.com/image/
245867500/?terms=%22Steven%20long%22%20%20Sandy%20creek&
match=1.

Effron, Seth. "Judge: naming of pot boat captain was improper,"
Tallahassee Democrat, February 14, 1978, 18, https://www.newspapers.
com/image/245857982/?terms=%22Steven%20long%22%20testi
mony%20Sandy%20creek&match=1.

Etters, Karl. "Man, 70, sentenced to death is paroled," Tallahassee Democrat, April 19, 2017, A1, https://www.newspapers.com/image/292805624/?terms=%22David%20Goodwin%22%20&match=1.

Fountain, Kimber. "High on High Island," 2021, 1-5, https://www.galvestonmonthly.com/history/cowboy-mafia.html.

Goodwin v. State, 1981FL 405, 55086 405 So. 2d. https://law.justia.com/cases/florida/supreme-court/1981/55086-0.html.

https://law.justia.com/cases/florida/supreme-court/1981/55086-0.html, 405 So. 2d 170 (1981), "Goodwin v. State, No. 55086

https://www.newspapers.com/image/5863948/?article=0c8a2186-1e29-4064-877c-96f9642beb51 obituary Paris News July 6,1989 page 2

Jackson, Orval. "Controversy Follows 'Sinkhole' Murders In Rural N. Florida," Miami Herald, January 15, 1978, 2, https://www.newspapers.com/image/627446560/?terms=Controversy%20follows%20Sinkhole%20a%20Murders%20in%20Rural.

Jackson, Orval. "Deadly Rendezvous: Couples, Smugglers Pick Same Spot," Miami Herald, January 15, 1978, 1, https://www.newspapers.com/image/627446560/?terms=Controversy%20follows%20Sinkhole%20a%20Murders%20in%20Rural.

Jackson, Orval. "Drug murders: FBI, Florida authorities accused with bungling case," News-Press, January 15, 1978, 5B, https://www.newspapers.com/image/212223142/?terms=Drug%20murders%20fbi&match=1.

MacFeely, F.T. "Tears Halt Sinkhole Death Trial," Florida Today, April 29, 1978, 4B, https://www.newspapers.com/image/124977995/?terms=Tears%20halt%20sinkhole%20&match=1.

MacFeely, F.T. "Vines recalls guarding Sinkhole victims," The Bradenton Herald, April 28, 1978, 17, https://www.newspapers.com/image/717997015/?terms=Vines%20recalls%20guarding%20&match=1.

Makeig, John. "Police know who blew man's face away but can't prove it," Fort Worth Star Telegram, October 10, 1978, B1, https://www.newspapers.com/image/634629450/?terms=Bill%20clifton&match=1.

McCarthy, Philip. "Nab Porno Guy With 75G Pills," Daily News, September 1, 1973, 5, https://www.newspapers.com/image/465516757/?terms=Nab%20porno%20%20guy&match=1.

Renner, Tom. "NY Crime Committee Starting Broad Probe," *Newsday* (Suffolk Edition), September 25, 1971, 9, https://www.news papers.com/image/719335401/?terms=Umbers%20crime%20commit tee%20probe&match=1.

Schlachter, Barry. "Money and passion," *Fort Worth Star Telegram*, April 30, 1989, 1, https://www.newspapers.com/image/641158111/? terms=Cauble&match=1.

Sentinel Star Services, "Prosecutor says Goodwin lured 3 to their deaths," *The Orlando Sentinel*. May 25, 1978, 2-C, https://www.newspa pers.com/image/300932605/?terms=Prosecutor%20says%20Good win%20&match=1.

Times news service, "State Probes FBI Charges," *The Chapel Hill Newspaper*, December 13, 1977, A1, https://www.newspapers.com/ image/783063081/?terms=%22Stephen%20long%22%20%22John% 20Mitchell%22%20fbi.

United States of America, Plaintiff-appellee, v. Rex C. Cauble, Individually and Doing Business As Cauble Enterprises, 1983 5th Cir., 706 F.2d 1322, https://law.justia.com/cases/federal/appellate-courts/F2/ 706/1322/378818/.

UPI, "Crime Unit Is Absolved In Murders," *The Tampa Tribune*, October 20, 1978, 6-B, https://www.newspapers.com/image/ 335430918/?terms=Crime%20unit%20absolved%20&match=1.

UPI, "Judge Ejects Reporters From Trial," *The Miami Herald*, September 18, 1979, 1, https://www.newspapers.com/image/ 628256081/?terms=Judge%20ejects%20reporters&match=.1.

Whitely, Michael. "Capo May have led two lives," *Tallahassee Democrat*, November 6, 1977, 26, https://www.newspapers.com/image/ 245893746/?terms=Capo%20may%20have%20led%20two%20lives& match=1.

Whitely, Michael. "Eight charged in sinkhole deaths," *Tallahassee Democrat*, October 19, 1977, 1, https://www.newspapers.com/image/ 245897843/?terms=Eight%20charged%20sinkhole%20&match=1.

Wilson, Gene. *The Cauble Connection: A Texas Scandal of Drugs, $ex and Greed*, Old Boston Publishers, Dallas Texas 2004.

Wireback, Howard. "Sentences given in sinkhole case," *Tallahassee Democrat*, April 6, 1978, 7, https://www.newspapers.com/image/

245801260/?terms=Lukefahr%20%20%20guilty%20Sandy%20creek& match=1.

Witt, Terry. "2 Murder Suspects Arraigned," *Panama City News-Herald*, December 4, 1977, 1, https://www.newspapers.com/iYmage/ 5121915/?terms=Suspects&match=1.

Witt, Terry. "Sinkhole Murder Probe Moves to Tallahassee," *Panama City News-Herald*, December 20, 1977, https://www.newspapers.com/ image/5127331/?terms=Sinkhole%20Murder%20probe%20moves% 20to%20Tallahassee%20&match=1.

Wright, Lawrence. "Rex Cauble and the Cowboy Mafia," *Texas Monthly*, November 1980, https://www.texasmonthly.com/true-crime/rex-cauble-and-the-cowboy-mafia/.

BIOGRAPHIES

Phil and Sandy Hamman are the authors of *Gitchie Girl, Gitchie Girl Uncovered,* and *Duct Tape Killer.* All three were national bestsellers in true crime. Sandy is an elementary special education teacher. Phil recently retired after teaching high school for forty years. They were married in 1984 and have been blessed with two children and four grandchildren.

Fred played high school basketball, and went on to become a member of his college's Hall of Fame after scoring 1,000 points and grabbing more than 1,000 rebounds. He began his professional career as an English teacher and coach, but a lifelong desire to be in law enforcement led him to accept an appointment as a Special Agent with the Drug Enforcement Administration during its infancy. Following academy training, Fred worked the remainder of his DEA career in the New York office. During this time he was in charge of numerous high-profile cases including the notorious "Cowboy Mafia" ring. On two separate occasions Fred received the DEA's coveted Sustained Superior Performance Award, the DEA's Special Achievement Award (twice), and commendations from the NYPD, NJ State Police, Bermuda Police, and the Department of British Customs. He was married 47 years to his college sweetheart, Ginger, and has a daughter and son. Now retired and no longer living on airplanes and out of motels, Fred enjoys spending time with his children and four grandchildren.

PHOTOS

Special Agent Fred Boff began his federal law enforcement career in 1970 before joining the Drug Enforcement Administration on its inception date of July 1, 1973. During his career, he initiated and was involved in many high-level national and international investigations including assignment by DEA headquarters as the supervisor of the multi-state Mobile Task Force that later evolved into the massive investigation that became known as the "Cowboy Mafia."

Everett "Hatch" Hatcher, Fred's partner and close friend. He gave the ultimate sacrifice to help keep America a better place to live.

Fred and wife Ginger were married 47 years before her death in 2016.

Fred and Ginger's children, David and Suzie. David went on to become a teacher and coach and has put together some of the top high school basketball teams in the country. Suzie became a successful attorney.

Good Luck Daddy.
We'll miss you!

One of the many notes Suzie snuck into her daddy's suitcase before he left on one of his frequent job assignments. Fred still keeps a stack of the notes, and treasures the memories.

Rex Cauble the "Old Man" came from humble beginnings and went on to become a self-made millionaire but lost most of his fortune after being sentenced for his part in the Cowboy Mafia. *(By artist Jim Villim)*

The marijuana and other drugs were brought into the United States on shrimp boats. The *Agnes Pauline* or "*Aggie*" had been under watch by Special Agents. Its crew was busted bringing in a load of marijuana, and this was the key in solidifying evidence against the Cowboy Mafia.

The FBI wanted poster for Charles Everett Hughes was distributed across the country.

Self-proclaimed godfather Muscles Foster was amazed the law took him at his word.

Charles "Muscles" Foster was heavily investigated as being a Cowboy Mafia kingpin. During his trial he used the insanity defense.

Smuggler Les Fuller's Marlboro Man image turned out to be a smoke screen.

Les Fuller "The Marlboro Man" was one of the crew members on the Agnes Pauline.

Fred and his team chased the *Hermit* for months before its crew was finally arrested. This is one of many cases Fred was assigned to that was not associated with the Cowboy Mafia.

Two of the many honors and awards Fred received for his service as a
Special Agent.

Fred was the case agent in charge, and after a bust is sitting next to a stack of hermetically sealed cans containing cocaine and heroin.

MORE FROM PHIL HAMMAN & SANDY HAMMAN

GITCHIE GIRL

The sound of snapping twigs closed in on the five teenagers enjoying an evening around a glowing campfire at Gitchie Manitou State Park. The night of music and laughter had taken a dark turn. Evil loomed just beyond the tree line, and before the night was over, one of the Midwest's most horrific mass murders had left its bloodstains spewed across the campsite. One managed to survive and would come to be known as the "Gitchie Girl." Harrowing memories of the terrifying crime sent her spiraling out of control, and she grasped at every avenue to rebuild her life. Can one man, a rescue dog, and a glimmer of faith salvage a broken soul? This true story will touch your heart and leave you cheering that good can prevail over the depravity of mankind.

DUCT TAPE KILLER

When Piper Streyle failed to show up for work, a coworker called her home. Piper's three-and-a-half-year-old daughter, Shaina, answered and said, "A mean man carried Mommy away." Then the line went dead.

Piper was the second woman to vanish.

An intensive search by an elite team of investigators uncovered a secret crime location, but the discovery of a nightshirt cut in half, a burnt candle, and a homemade bondage board revealed the chilling truth behind the missing women. With the help of a quick-witted and streetwise maximum security prison inmate, prosecutor Larry Long and his team were able to piece together the sinister facts of the diabolical crimes.

HISTRIA
BOOKS

HISTRIA PERSPECTIVES

HISTRIA PERSPECTIVES
BOOKS TO CHALLENGE AND ENLIGHTEN

A.K. BRACKOB
DRACUL
OF THE FATHER

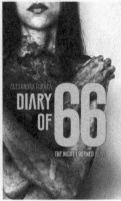

ALEXANDRA FURNEA
DIARY OF 66
THE NIGHT I BURNED ALIVE

THE BRANCHES
we
CHERISH
AN OPEN ADOPTION MEMOIR

LINDA R. SEXTON

OLIVIA GOODREAU
BUT SHE LOOKS FINE
FROM ILLNESS TO ACTIVISM

THE SILVER BULLET SOLUTION
IS IT TIME TO END THE WAR ON DRUGS?

JAMES E. GIERACH

NETWORKS RISING
THINKING TOGETHER IN A FLATTER WORLD

CHRISTOPHER BURNS

FOR THESE AND OTHER GREAT BOOKS VISIT
HISTRIABOOKS.COM